BEAR MARKET MILLIONAIRE: 42 BULLETPROOF STRATEGIES TO PROFIT FROM CRASHES, RECESSIONS, AND ECONOMIC CHAOS

MICHAEL FINK

CONTENTS

Front Matter:	1
SECTION I: MINDSET & PREPARATION	5
Chapter 2: The Psychology of Crisis Investing	9
Chapter 3: Economic Downturns – A Historical Perspective	15
Chapter 4: Building Your Financial Fortress Before the Storm	21
Chapter 5: The Power of Cash – Why Dry Powder Wins Recessions	27
SECTION II: STRATEGIC FRAMEWORK FOR BEAR MARKET PROFITS	33
Chapter 7: Defensive vs. Offensive Strategies in a Downturn	40
Chapter 8: The Role of Fear and Greed – Spotting Market Sentiment Shifts	46
SECTION III: STOCK MARKET STRATEGIES DURING A CRASH	52
Chapter 10: Dividend Stocks – Passive Income in a Recession	59
Chapter 11: The Short Selling Playbook – Profiting from Falling Stocks	65
Chapter 12: Defensive Sectors & "Recession-Proof" Stocks	72
SECTION IV: ALTERNATIVE INVESTMENTS & HEDGING STRATEGIES	79
Chapter 14: Bonds & Fixed Income for Stability	86
Chapter 15: Crypto in a Bear Market – Opportunity or Trap?	93
Chapter 16: Options Trading for Downturns – Hedging & Speculating	100

📌 SECTION V: REAL ESTATE & BUSINESS STRATEGIES IN ECONOMIC CHAOS — 107

Chapter 18: Investing in REITs – A Passive Approach to Bear Market Real Estate — 115

Chapter 19: Mastering the Bear Market Mindset – How to Stay Rational When Others Panic — 123

📌 SECTION VI: CASE STUDIES & EXECUTION PLAN — 129

Chapter 21: The 42 Bulletproof Strategies Checklist — 137

Chapter 22: Creating Your Bear Market Action Plan – Step-by-Step Guide to Profiting in Downturns — 144

Chapter 23: Avoiding Common Mistakes & Psychological Pitfalls — 151

Chapter 24: Preparing for the Next Recession—Today — 159

Chapter 25: Final Words – Turning Chaos into Wealth — 167

FRONT MATTER:

Copyright Notice

All rights reserved. No part of this book may be copied, reproduced, stored in a retrieval system, or shared in any form—electronic, mechanical, photocopying, recording, or otherwise—without the prior written permission of the author or publisher. Unauthorized duplication or distribution of this book or any portion of it is strictly prohibited and may result in legal action.

The author and publisher have made every effort to ensure the accuracy and completeness of the content provided herein. However, neither the author nor the publisher assumes any responsibility for errors, inaccuracies, or omissions. This book is provided "as is" without any warranties of any kind, either express or implied. The strategies, techniques, and methodologies outlined in this book are based on the author's research, opinions, and experience and are subject to change as market conditions evolve.

Any trademarks, registered trademarks, or company names mentioned in this book are the property of their respective owners. The inclusion of such names or marks does not imply endorsement or affiliation.

Disclaimer

The information presented in *Bear Market Millionaire: 42 Bulletproof Strategies to Profit from Crashes, Recessions, and Economic Chaos* is for **educational and informational purposes only**. This book is **not financial, investment, legal, tax, or accounting advice** and should not be construed as such. Readers are advised to conduct their own research and consult with **a licensed financial advisor, CPA, or legal professional** before making any investment decisions.

The strategies and concepts discussed in this book are based on historical data, personal experiences, and industry knowledge. However, **past performance is not indicative of future results**. The author does not guarantee any particular outcome, profit, or return on investment. Markets are **unpredictable, volatile, and inherently risky**, and any investment carries the potential for financial loss.

By reading this book, you acknowledge and agree that the author and publisher are not responsible for any financial or investment decisions you make based on the information presented. **You assume full responsibility for any risks and financial losses that may result from your investment choices.**

Additionally, the case studies and success stories provided in this book are for illustrative purposes only. Individual results will vary based on **market conditions, timing, personal risk tolerance, and financial goals**. Always **conduct your due**

diligence and consider seeking professional guidance tailored to your unique financial situation.

Risk Warning

Investing in financial markets, particularly during **bear markets, recessions, and periods of economic turbulence**, carries **significant risks**. While economic downturns can present unique opportunities for wealth-building, **no strategy is foolproof**. Even seasoned investors with extensive experience can suffer losses in volatile markets.

Key risks include but are not limited to:

• **Stock Market Risk** – Equities can decline rapidly due to economic instability, poor corporate earnings, geopolitical events, or market sentiment shifts.

• **Liquidity Risk** – During bear markets, selling assets at a favorable price may be difficult, leading to potential losses.

• **Interest Rate Risk** – Fluctuating interest rates can impact the performance of stocks, bonds, real estate, and other asset classes.

• **Credit Risk** – Companies may default on debt, leading to losses for bondholders and investors.

• **Macroeconomic Risk** – Recessions, inflation, deflation, and policy changes can heavily influence investment outcomes.

• **Psychological Risk** – Emotional decision-making, panic selling, and herd mentality often lead to costly mistakes.

Readers must be aware that **market downturns can last longer and be more severe than expected**. While some investors thrive in these conditions, others may **incur signifi-**

cant financial losses if they fail to properly manage risk, maintain liquidity, or implement sound investment strategies.

PROCEED WITH CAUTION. Never invest money you cannot afford to lose, and always consider how potential losses may impact your financial well-being. Thoughtful risk management, continuous education, and a disciplined investment approach are critical to navigating bear markets successfully.

With this in mind, let's explore the strategies, mindsets, and investment techniques that can **help you capitalize on bear markets while minimizing risk**. If approached correctly, economic downturns can present some of the **greatest opportunities for building lasting wealth**.

Now, let's begin.

📌 SECTION I: MINDSET & PREPARATION

CHAPTER 1: INTRODUCTION – WHY BEAR MARKETS CREATE MILLIONAIRES

"*Be fearful when others are greedy, and greedy when others are fearful.*" – *Warren Buffett*

The Wealth-Building Advantage of Market Chaos

Every economic crisis brings stories of financial devastation—businesses failing, portfolios shrinking, and retirements delayed. But what's often overlooked is the *other side* of the equation: the people who capitalize on these downturns and emerge wealthier than ever. The reality is that **some of the greatest fortunes in history have been made during bear markets, recessions, and economic collapses.**

Take the 2008 financial crisis. While millions lost their savings and homes, investors like Michael Burry, John Paulson, and Warren Buffett saw an opportunity. They understood that markets are cyclical, and downturns—while painful—offer once-in-a-generation chances to acquire assets at deeply discounted prices.

The same pattern has played out time and time again. Whether it was the Great Depression, the dot-com crash, or the COVID-19 market plunge, **investors who remained calm, strategically positioned their capital, and embraced a contrarian mindset walked away as winners.**

Understanding Market Cycles & Downturn Psychology

Before we dive into the 42 bulletproof strategies for profiting in a bear market, it's crucial to understand why these financial downturns happen and, more importantly, why most people fail to take advantage of them.

1. Market Cycles: The Inevitable Boom and Bust

Markets **do not move in a straight line**. They go through predictable cycles of expansion, peak, contraction, and recovery:

✅ **Boom Phase:** Economic optimism drives asset prices up. Businesses expand, credit is easy to access, and investors feel invincible.

🚀 **Peak Phase:** Valuations become excessive, fueled by speculation and irrational exuberance. Think of the 1999 dot-com bubble or 2007's housing mania.

📉 **Bear Market & Recession Phase:** The bubble bursts, panic sets in, and prices crash. The economy slows, layoffs surge, and fear grips investors.

📈 **Recovery & Bull Market:** After hitting rock bottom, markets stabilize, innovation continues, and a new cycle of growth begins.

While each cycle varies in length and intensity, **one thing remains constant: bear markets do not last forever**. And for those who are prepared, these downturns offer the best buying opportunities of a lifetime.

2. Why Most Investors Panic and Sell at the Worst Time

When markets crash, human psychology kicks in. Fear takes over. **The pain of losing money is psychologically twice as powerful as the pleasure of gaining it**, which explains why so many investors panic-sell at market bottoms—right before the recovery starts.

Here's why most people fail in bear markets:

• **They Buy High & Sell Low:** The average investor piles into stocks at the peak of euphoria and dumps them when fear is at its highest.

• **They Follow the Herd:** Seeing others panic and sell reinforces the belief that the market will keep collapsing.

• **They React Emotionally:** Instead of thinking strategically, they let fear dictate their decisions.

• **They Lack Liquidity:** Without cash on hand, they can't take advantage of discounted assets.

3. The Contrarian Investor's Edge

The secret to **becoming a bear market millionaire** is simple but difficult to execute: **do the opposite of what most investors do.**

• When people are **selling in a panic**, you should be **buying quality assets at a discount**.

• When people are **hoarding cash out of fear**, you should be **positioning yourself for the next bull market**.

- When people **chase trends at all-time highs**, you should be **patiently waiting for better entry points**.

This is easier said than done because **going against the crowd is psychologically uncomfortable**. But this is what separates the average investor from the elite wealth-builders who thrive during economic downturns.

What This Book Will Teach You

Over the next 24 chapters, I'll walk you through the **exact playbook that smart investors use to profit from bear markets.**

☑ **We'll cover time-tested investing strategies** that have created wealth in every major downturn.

☑ **We'll dive into actionable, step-by-step frameworks** for spotting opportunities, minimizing risk, and maximizing returns.

☑ **We'll break down real-world case studies** of investors who turned crises into fortunes—and the lessons you can apply today.

By the time you finish this book, you'll **see bear markets not as something to fear, but as the biggest wealth-building opportunity of your lifetime.**

Let's get started.

CHAPTER 2: THE PSYCHOLOGY OF CRISIS INVESTING

"The investor's chief problem—and even his worst enemy—is likely to be himself."

— Benjamin Graham

Why Bear Markets Trigger Fear and Irrational Decision-Making

Imagine you've built a solid investment portfolio over the years. You've studied the markets, made informed decisions, and watched your wealth grow. Then, seemingly out of nowhere, the market crashes. The news is filled with apocalyptic headlines—"Worst Stock Market Drop in Decades!" "Investors Panic as Markets Plummet!"—and your portfolio is bleeding red.

What do you do?

Most investors panic. They log into their brokerage accounts and hit the sell button. The fear of watching their investments drop further is unbearable. They rationalize that it's better to "cut losses now" than to "lose everything."

The irony? **This is exactly the wrong move.**

Market crashes are terrifying because they trigger a **primal fear response**—the same one our ancestors relied on to survive in the wild. Our brains evolved to avoid immediate pain and uncertainty. When we see prices falling and people panicking, we instinctively want to flee.

But successful investing isn't about **reacting emotionally**—it's about **thinking strategically**. Bear markets are where millionaires are made, not by those who run from the storm, but by those who navigate through it.

The Three Psychological Traps That Destroy Investors

During downturns, three major psychological traps prevent investors from making rational decisions:

1. Loss Aversion: Why the Pain of Losing Feels Twice as Bad

Psychologists have found that **losing money is twice as painful as gaining the same amount is pleasurable**. This means a 30% drop in your portfolio feels significantly worse than the joy of a 30% gain.

Because of this, many investors make the **worst possible decision at the worst possible time**—they sell after a crash, locking in their losses instead of waiting for the eventual recovery.

Smart Investors Do This Instead:

• They accept that losses on paper are **not the same as actual losses** unless they sell.

• They focus on **long-term value**, not short-term price fluctuations.

- They buy more when **assets are discounted** instead of panic-selling.

2. Herd Mentality: Following the Crowd Into Disaster

During a crisis, humans look to others for cues on how to react. If everyone else is panicking, selling, and assuming the market will never recover, it *must* be the right move, right?

Wrong.

Markets are driven by mass psychology. Fear is contagious. When people panic and sell, it fuels further panic and selling, causing an accelerating market crash. Those who act rationally **against the crowd** stand to benefit the most.

Smart Investors Do This Instead:

- They recognize that **when everyone is selling, it's often a buying opportunity**.

- They look at **fundamentals**, not crowd-driven fear.

- They resist making investment decisions based on news headlines and emotional reactions.

3. Recency Bias: Assuming the Crash Will Never End

When a bear market drags on, investors start to believe **it will last forever**. This psychological bias—where recent events feel more significant than historical trends—causes people to assume markets will keep crashing indefinitely.

But here's the truth: **Markets always recover.**

Every bear market in history has eventually turned into a bull market. Yet, in the middle of the storm, most investors fail to see past the immediate crisis.

Smart Investors Do This Instead:

• They remind themselves that **bear markets are temporary**.

• They review historical charts to see that **every crash has led to recovery**.

• They build a strategy that **takes advantage of cheap assets before the rebound**.

How to Cultivate an "Anti-Fragile" Mindset in Bear Markets

Now that you understand the psychological traps, how do you override them and position yourself for success? The key is to develop an **anti-fragile mindset**—one that doesn't just survive economic downturns but thrives in them.

1. Reframe Fear as Opportunity

Instead of viewing bear markets as catastrophic, see them as **massive wealth-building opportunities**. The most successful investors, from Warren Buffett to Ray Dalio, have built fortunes by capitalizing on downturns.

Whenever the market crashes, ask yourself:

✅ *What assets can I buy at a discount right now?*

✅ *How can I position myself for the inevitable recovery?*

✅ *What is the market overreacting to—and how can I profit from it?*

2. Adopt a Long-Term Perspective

If you look at any stock market chart over the past 100 years, you'll notice one thing: despite all the crashes, corrections, and recessions, **the overall trajectory is up**.

Wealth is built over decades, not days. If you focus on **long-term value creation**, short-term volatility becomes irrelevant.

3. Keep Dry Powder Ready (Liquidity is King)

Bear markets present **rare buying opportunities**, but only for those who have cash available. While others are forced to sell assets at a loss, **having liquidity allows you to buy quality investments at a steep discount**.

Your strategy:

• Keep a **portion of your portfolio in cash** to seize opportunities.

• Avoid overleveraging—debt can force you to sell at the worst time.

• Prepare ahead of time instead of reacting after the crash.

4. Master Emotional Control

Emotional resilience is one of the greatest assets in investing. The ability to remain calm, logical, and strategic when others are panicking is what sets successful investors apart.

Ways to strengthen emotional control:

• Turn off financial news when markets crash—it only fuels fear.

• Develop **rules-based investing** to remove emotions from decision-making.

- Have a **written game plan** before a crash occurs so you act rationally.

My Thoughts: Thinking Like a Crisis Investor

If you want to become a **bear market millionaire**, you need to think differently than the average investor. You must **override fear, break free from herd mentality, and develop an anti-fragile mindset.**

Bear markets will always happen. Recessions will come and go. **Your ability to capitalize on them will determine whether you emerge stronger—or become just another casualty.**

In the next chapter, we'll dive into **how to prepare your finances before a downturn happens**—so when the next crash comes, you'll be ready to profit while everyone else panics.

CHAPTER 3: ECONOMIC DOWNTURNS – A HISTORICAL PERSPECTIVE

"*History doesn't repeat itself, but it often rhymes.*"
— Mark Twain

Lessons from the Past: How Crashes Shape the Future

If you want to understand **how to profit from bear markets**, you need to study the past. Economic downturns, recessions, and market crashes aren't random; they follow **predictable patterns**, and those who recognize them can position themselves to profit.

Every financial crisis has two types of investors:

• **The victims**—those who panic, sell at the worst time, and lose money.

• **The opportunists**—those who prepare, buy undervalued assets, and emerge wealthier than before.

So, how do you become part of the second group? **By studying history, identifying patterns, and learning from the investors who turned past downturns into fortunes.**

Major Bear Markets and Their Lessons

1. The Great Depression (1929-1939) – The Ultimate Market Collapse

📉 **What Happened?**

• The **1920s stock market boom** led to rampant speculation. Stocks were bought on **margin** (borrowed money), creating an inflated bubble.

• In **October 1929**, the bubble burst, leading to the **worst market crash in U.S. history**.

• Stock prices **plummeted by over 85%**, wiping out millions of investors.

• Banks failed, businesses collapsed, and unemployment soared.

📈 **Key Lessons for Investors:**

✅ **Avoid overleveraging** – Many investors were using borrowed money, amplifying their losses. **Debt kills in a downturn.**

✅ **Cash is king** – Those with liquidity bought assets at fire-sale prices, making fortunes.

✅ **Market recoveries take time** – While the Great Depression lasted a decade, investors who bought after the crash saw **huge returns in the 1940s and beyond**.

2. The 1973-1974 Oil Crisis – Inflation and Stagflation

📉 **What Happened?**

• The **oil embargo** by OPEC led to skyrocketing energy prices and inflation.

Bear Market Millionaire: 42 Bulletproof Strategies to Profit from ...

- The **stock market dropped nearly 50%**, and economic growth stagnated.

- **Unemployment and inflation rose simultaneously**—a phenomenon called **stagflation**.

✓ **Key Lessons for Investors:**

✅ **Commodities hedge against inflation** – Gold, oil, and real assets **outperformed stocks** in this period.

✅ **High-inflation environments hurt traditional portfolios** – Investors must **diversify beyond stocks** in high-inflation times.

3. The Dot-Com Bubble Burst (2000-2002) – The Tech Collapse

📉 **What Happened?**

- The late 1990s saw an explosion of internet-based companies. Valuations skyrocketed despite **many companies having zero revenue**.

- In **2000, the bubble burst**, wiping out $5 trillion in market value.

- Many tech companies went bankrupt, while **only the strongest survived (Amazon, Apple, Google, etc.).**

✓ **Key Lessons for Investors:**

✅ **Don't chase hype stocks** – Companies with no profits eventually collapse. Fundamentals matter.

✅ **Quality companies survive downturns** – Amazon lost **over 90% of its stock value** but later became one of the biggest companies in history.

☑ **Bear markets filter out weak businesses** – Recessions are a test of strength. Only the best companies make it.

4. The 2008 Financial Crisis – The Housing Bubble Burst

📉 **What Happened?**

• Banks gave out risky mortgages to **unqualified buyers**, creating a housing market bubble.

• When the bubble burst, home values crashed, and **banks collapsed**.

• The stock market **dropped over 50%**, and the global economy went into recession.

📈 **Key Lessons for Investors:**

☑ **Debt-fueled bubbles always burst** – When people overextend on credit, a crash is inevitable.

☑ **Government bailouts impact markets** – The Federal Reserve **intervened**, leading to **a decade-long bull market after the crash**.

☑ **Fortunes were made by those who saw it coming** – Investors like **Michael Burry and Warren Buffett bought assets at extreme discounts** and made billions.

5. The COVID-19 Crash (2020) – The Fastest Market Recovery in History

📉 **What Happened?**

• The global pandemic **shut down economies overnight**, leading to a **record-breaking stock market crash** in March 2020.

- Governments **pumped trillions of dollars** into the economy, leading to a **V-shaped recovery**.

- **Tech stocks soared**, while traditional industries (travel, hospitality) suffered.

📈 **Key Lessons for Investors:**

✅ **Massive government stimulus changes market behavior** – The stock market rebounded faster than expected due to central bank intervention.

✅ **Tech and innovation thrive in crises** – Companies like Zoom, Tesla, and Amazon **skyrocketed in value**.

✅ **Bear markets can be short-lived** – Unlike the Great Depression, this crash lasted only a few months.

Common Investor Mistakes in Past Crashes

Looking at history, **the biggest mistakes investors make during downturns** include:

❌ **Selling at the bottom** – Panic-selling locks in losses, while patient investors see recoveries.

❌ **Ignoring fundamentals** – Buying overhyped assets without revenue (dot-com, crypto bubbles) leads to disaster.

❌ **Overleveraging** – Taking on **too much debt before a crash** can wipe out an entire portfolio.

❌ **Lack of diversification** – Investors who were **100% in one asset class (stocks, crypto, real estate) suffered the worst losses**.

. . .

My Opinion: How to Use History to Your Advantage

If there's **one thing I've learned** from studying market history, it's this: **every crash is an opportunity for those who stay rational.**

📌 **The majority of people panic, but the smartest investors see opportunity.**

📌 **Bear markets wipe out speculation and reward disciplined investors.**

📌 **Government policies, inflation, and economic shifts create cycles that repeat over time.**

While **no two bear markets are the same**, they all follow a **predictable pattern**:

🚀 **Euphoria → Overconfidence → Crash → Panic → Recovery → Growth.**

The key is to **recognize where we are in the cycle** and position yourself accordingly.

In the next chapter, we'll cover **how to build a financial fortress before the next economic downturn**—because the best time to prepare isn't after the crash... it's *before it happens*.

CHAPTER 4: BUILDING YOUR FINANCIAL FORTRESS BEFORE THE STORM

"*Only when the tide goes out do you discover who's been swimming naked.*"
— Warren Buffett

Why You Need to Prepare Before the Next Bear Market

Every economic downturn reveals a hard truth: **most people are financially unprepared for crises.**

When recessions hit, jobs are lost, investments shrink, and panic sets in. Those who **failed to prepare** are left scrambling—selling assets at a loss, struggling to pay bills, and watching their wealth evaporate.

But there's another group: **the prepared investors.** They **don't panic**—they take advantage. They **have liquidity** to buy undervalued assets. They **have low debt** and strong cash flow, allowing them to weather the storm without stress.

The difference? **Preparation.**

In this chapter, we'll cover the **five key steps** to **build a financial fortress** so you can survive—and thrive—during the next downturn.

Step 1: Strengthening Your Cash Flow and Emergency Fund

The first rule of bear market survival is simple: **cash is king.**

In an economic crisis, liquidity (having available cash) gives you:

☑ The ability to **cover living expenses without panic**

☑ The flexibility to **buy assets when they are undervalued**

☑ Protection from **unexpected job loss or business downturns**

How Much Cash Should You Have?

A standard rule is to **have at least 6-12 months of living expenses saved in cash.** However, if you're an investor looking to seize bear market opportunities, you may want **even more liquidity** to buy stocks, real estate, or businesses at a discount.

Where to Store Cash Safely:

- **High-yield savings accounts** (FDIC insured)

- **Money market funds**

- **Short-term U.S. Treasury bills** (low-risk and liquid)

What Not to Do:

✘ Don't keep too much cash in low-interest accounts that lose value due to inflation.

✘ Don't invest your emergency fund in risky assets—you need this money to be **accessible**.

Step 2: Eliminating Bad Debt (Because Debt Can Destroy You in a Recession)

Debt is like **an anchor**—it's easy to carry when the economy is strong, but in a recession, it can **drag you down fast.**

Good Debt vs. Bad Debt:

✅ **Good debt** – Low-interest loans that finance appreciating assets (real estate, businesses, investments).

✘ **Bad debt** – High-interest consumer debt (credit cards, car loans, personal loans) that drains wealth.

How to Reduce Debt Before a Bear Market:

1️⃣ **Pay off high-interest credit cards first** – These are the biggest wealth destroyers.

2️⃣ **Refinance loans while interest rates are low** – Lock in lower rates before a recession hits.

3️⃣ **Avoid taking on new unnecessary debt** – If a downturn comes, you don't want high fixed payments draining your cash flow.

What Not to Do:

✘ Don't rely on **future income** to pay off debt—economic slowdowns can disrupt income sources.

✖ Don't ignore debt until the crisis hits—**it will be too late by then.**

Step 3: Maintaining Multiple Income Streams

One of the worst things that can happen in a recession? **Losing your only source of income.**

Most people rely on **a single paycheck**, which makes them vulnerable when layoffs surge. The wealthiest investors **diversify their income sources** so they are never reliant on just one.

How to Build Multiple Income Streams:

📌 **Invest in dividend stocks** – Passive income from solid, recession-resistant companies.

📌 **Start an online business** – E-commerce, consulting, or digital products that generate extra cash.

📌 **Buy rental properties** – Real estate cash flow can provide stability during downturns.

📌 **Freelance or side hustle** – A second income stream reduces financial risk.

Step 4: Preparing an Investment Strategy for a Bear Market

When a downturn hits, **you want to be in a position to buy undervalued assets**, not panic-sell like the masses. That means having a **clear investment strategy before the crash happens.**

Investment Rules for Bear Markets:

☑ **Recession-proof your portfolio** – Focus on **defensive stocks** (healthcare, utilities, consumer staples).

☑ **Have cash ready** – Bear markets create **incredible buying opportunities.**

☑ **Look for value, not hype** – During downturns, high-quality companies get mispriced. That's your chance to buy them at a discount.

☑ **Consider alternative assets** – Precious metals, bonds, and real estate can hedge against volatility.

Step 5: Protecting Yourself Against the Unexpected

A financial crisis can come from anywhere— **job loss, medical emergencies, inflation spikes, or even geopolitical events.** To protect yourself, you need to have **defensive measures in place.**

Key Defensive Moves:

📌 **Health and disability insurance** – Protect your income in case of illness or injury.

📌 **Diversify your assets** – Don't keep all your money in one investment type.

📌 **Have a recession plan** – Know what steps you'll take if your income drops by 50%.

. . .

What's Next? Positioning Yourself for Bear Market Profits

Once you've built your financial fortress, you're ready for the **next stage**: taking advantage of market downturns to build wealth.

In the next chapter, we'll dive into **why holding cash is a competitive advantage in bear markets**—and how to use it to buy undervalued assets while others are panicking.

My Opinion

From everything I've seen in bear markets, the people who **win big** are the ones who prepared long before the crisis hit. Those who panic, sell at a loss, and scramble for cash always regret not taking action earlier.

I believe that **financial preparation isn't just about surviving downturns—it's about turning them into opportunities**. If you have cash, low debt, and a solid investment plan, you'll see bear markets differently: not as threats, but as rare chances to **buy assets at massive discounts**.

Too many people **ignore preparation until it's too late**. In my opinion, **waiting until a recession hits is the worst financial mistake you can make**. The time to prepare is **now** —before the next downturn arrives.

CHAPTER 5: THE POWER OF CASH – WHY DRY POWDER WINS RECESSIONS

"*Cash combined with courage in a crisis is priceless."*

— Warren Buffett

Why Cash Is the Most Underrated Asset in a Bear Market

During bull markets, cash is seen as a **lazy asset**—something that earns little interest while stocks, crypto, and real estate skyrocket in value. Investors chase high returns, dumping their cash reserves into riskier assets, believing they are "missing out" by holding liquidity.

Then the bear market arrives.

Suddenly, those who laughed at cash are **desperate to get their hands on it**. As asset prices collapse, credit tightens, and fear takes over, investors realize that **having cash in a crisis is a superpower**. Those who have it **can buy distressed assets, negotiate better deals, and avoid being forced to sell at the worst time**.

This chapter explains why **liquidity is king in a recession**, how to build a strategic cash position, and how to use it to **capitalize on bear market opportunities** while others panic.

The Three Reasons Cash Wins in a Bear Market

1. Cash Buys Undervalued Assets

History has proven that bear markets offer some of the **greatest buying opportunities in investing**. Stocks, real estate, and businesses that were overpriced just months before suddenly become **deeply discounted**.

Examples of How Cash Created Wealth in a Crisis:

✅ **2008 Financial Crisis:** Investors who had cash bought stocks like Apple ($12), Amazon ($35), and JPMorgan Chase ($15) before they skyrocketed in the recovery.

✅ **COVID-19 Market Crash (2020):** Stocks plummeted 30-50% in weeks. Investors with cash scooped up bargains, profiting when the market rebounded.

✅ **Real Estate Crashes:** Those with cash during housing downturns buy prime properties at **huge discounts**, while overleveraged investors are forced to sell.

In every bear market, **the wealth shifts from those who are overleveraged to those who are liquid**.

2. Cash Protects You from Forced Selling

When recessions hit, people with **too much debt and not enough liquidity** are forced to sell assets—usually at massive losses—to cover expenses.

🚩 **Why Forced Selling Is Dangerous:**

- Stocks and real estate are **worth much less in a crash** than in a strong economy. Selling at the bottom locks in losses.

- Banks reduce credit limits, meaning **loans that were once available may disappear overnight**.

- Many businesses and investors **are wiped out simply because they run out of cash**, not because their assets were bad investments.

Having a **strong cash reserve** prevents you from becoming a victim of the downturn. **It gives you breathing room to make smart decisions instead of reacting out of desperation.**

3. Cash Is a Negotiation Weapon

In a bear market, **cash gives you power**. When others are struggling to stay afloat, cash-rich investors can:

📌 **Buy stocks at their lowest valuations** in years.

📌 **Purchase real estate at bargain prices** from motivated sellers.

📌 **Invest in distressed businesses** that need liquidity to survive.

📌 **Negotiate better deals**—cash buyers often get discounts compared to those relying on financing.

Having cash when others are desperate gives you **leverage**. Instead of begging for deals, you **dictate terms**.

. . .

How to Build and Maintain a Strategic Cash Reserve

Since cash **loses value to inflation over time**, most investors hesitate to hold large cash positions. However, the key isn't to sit on cash forever—it's to **have it available at the right time.**

How Much Cash Should You Hold?

◆ **For emergency purposes** – 6-12 months of living expenses.

◆ **For investment opportunities** – 10-30% of your portfolio in liquid assets.

◆ **If you expect a bear market** – Increase cash reserves to **30-50%**, depending on risk tolerance.

The goal isn't to hold cash forever but to deploy it when assets go on sale.

Best Places to Hold Cash for Bear Market Readiness

✅ **High-yield savings accounts** – Keeps funds liquid while earning some interest.

✅ **Money market funds** – Low-risk, short-term investments that keep cash accessible.

✅ **Short-term U.S. Treasury bills** – Risk-free and provide a hedge against market volatility.

✅ **Gold or precious metals** – Not cash, but acts as a store of value during crises.

🚫 **What Not to Do:**

✘ **Holding too much cash in low-interest accounts** that lose purchasing power to inflation.

✘ **Keeping all cash in a single bank**—diversify across accounts in case of banking issues.

Deploying Cash at the Right Time: The 3-Phase Approach

Simply **holding cash isn't enough**—you need a plan for **when and how to deploy it.**

Phase 1: Prepare for a Market Crash (Early Bear Market)

📌 Build cash reserves before a downturn happens.

📌 Start researching assets that could be **undervalued in a crash**.

📌 Avoid unnecessary spending and high-risk investments.

Phase 2: Buy Assets During Maximum Fear (Market Bottom)

📌 Look for **fundamentally strong stocks** trading at historic lows.

📌 **Buy real estate** from distressed sellers at discount prices.

📌 **Negotiate aggressively**—in downturns, cash buyers get the best deals.

Phase 3: Ride the Recovery (Bull Market Begins)

📌 Gradually reduce cash holdings as **assets appreciate**.

📌 Rebalance portfolio to **maximize long-term growth**.

📌 Stay prepared—another downturn will eventually come.

My Opinion

After observing countless bear markets, **one thing is crystal clear**—cash is the most powerful tool an investor can have when recessions hit. **Most people don't realize this until it's too late.**

In my opinion, the biggest mistake **retail investors make** is staying fully invested at all times. While holding cash **feels like missing out during a bull run**, it becomes **invaluable when the market crashes** and bargains appear everywhere.

Those who **mock cash as a "wasted asset"** are usually the same ones **begging for liquidity when markets tank**. I've learned that the best investors **always have cash reserves ready**—because while others panic, they're preparing to buy.

If you want to be a **bear market millionaire**, you need to **think differently** than the crowd. That means **holding cash when it's unpopular** and **deploying it when everyone else is afraid**.

In the next chapter, we'll dive into **how to read market cycles and identify when to buy and sell**—because timing is everything when it comes to investing in bear markets.

📌 SECTION II: STRATEGIC FRAMEWORK FOR BEAR MARKET PROFITS

CHAPTER 6: UNDERSTANDING MARKET CYCLES & TIMING

"Markets go up and down, but they don't move randomly. They follow cycles, and the best investors know when to strike."

— Michael Fink

Why Market Cycles Matter

One of the biggest mistakes investors make is **treating every market movement as unpredictable chaos**. But the truth is, markets move in **cycles**—and those who understand these cycles have a massive advantage.

Booms and busts **are not random**. They follow **predictable phases**, driven by economic trends, investor psychology, and government policies. If you know what phase we're in, you can:

✅ **Avoid buying at market tops when risk is highest.**

✅ **Buy undervalued assets at market bottoms.**

✅ **Hold cash and wait when markets are overheated.**

☑ **Ignore media hype and invest based on fundamentals.**

This chapter will break down **how to read market cycles, identify key indicators of market tops and bottoms, and develop the patience to strike at the right time.**

The Four Phases of a Market Cycle

Every market—stocks, real estate, crypto—moves through **four main phases**:

1. Accumulation Phase (Smart Money Moves In)

• The economy is recovering from a recession.

• Most investors are still fearful, but **smart money is quietly buying undervalued assets**.

• Stock prices are low, and **there is little hype**.

• Economic indicators start improving.

☑ **Best strategy:** Accumulate quality assets before the bull market begins.

2. Markup Phase (Bull Market Takes Off)

• More investors realize the economy is improving.

• Stocks **steadily rise**, and optimism increases.

• Institutional investors and hedge funds buy aggressively.

• The media starts covering market gains, drawing in retail investors.

☑ **Best strategy:** Ride the trend but start taking some profits as valuations rise.

3. Distribution Phase (Euphoria & Market Tops)

- **Markets hit record highs, and everyone is bullish.**

- Stocks are overvalued, and speculation is rampant.

- Retail investors flood the market, believing the good times will last forever.

- Smart money starts selling.

⚠️ **Warning:** This is where most people **get greedy and buy at the top**—right before the crash.

✅ **Best strategy:** Reduce risk, hold cash, and avoid over-leveraging.

4. Markdown Phase (The Bear Market & Panic Selling)

- Markets begin declining, but **investors believe it's temporary**.

- As losses grow, panic sets in, and people sell at the worst time.

- Recession fears grow, and the media predicts economic doom.

- **Smart investors start buying again** as assets become undervalued.

✅ **Best strategy:** Stay calm, buy at discounts, and wait for the next bull market.

. . .

How Economic Indicators Signal Market Tops & Bottoms

You don't need a **crystal ball** to see where we are in the market cycle—just **follow the data**.

Indicators of Market Tops (Time to Reduce Risk & Hold Cash)

▶ **Unemployment is at record lows.** Everyone has a job, and the economy seems unstoppable.

▶ **Stock valuations are at extreme highs.** Price-to-earnings (P/E) ratios are unsustainable.

▶ **Retail investors are euphoric.** If everyone is bragging about stocks, we're near the top.

▶ **The Fed is raising interest rates.** Higher borrowing costs slow down economic growth.

▶ **Credit is easy to get.** When banks lend money to anyone, it's a bubble waiting to pop.

Indicators of Market Bottoms (Time to Buy & Strike)

☑ **Unemployment is rising.** Recessions bring layoffs, but this means we're near the bottom.

☑ **Stock prices are undervalued.** Blue-chip stocks are trading at deep discounts.

☑ **Panic is everywhere.** If people say, "It's different this time" and believe markets will never recover, it's time to buy.

☑ **The Fed is cutting interest rates.** Lower rates signal that the economy is about to recover.

✅ **Big investors are buying again.** Watch insider buying and hedge fund activity.

📌 **Rule of thumb:** *When the media says, "This time is different," history shows it never is.*

The Difference Between Corrections, Recessions, and Depressions

Not every market downturn is the same. Knowing the difference helps you react correctly:

Market Correction (Short-Term Pullback, -10% to -20%)

• Happens every 1-2 years.

• Often triggered by **profit-taking or short-term fears** (inflation, elections, geopolitical events).

• Markets **typically recover within months**.

✅ **Strategy:** Stay invested. Corrections are healthy.

Recession (Longer-Term Bear Market, -20% to -50%)

• Usually lasts **12-24 months**.

• Economic slowdown, rising unemployment, and declining corporate profits.

• **Stock markets drop 20-50%**, wiping out speculative gains.

• Creates **huge buying opportunities** for long-term investors.

✅ **Strategy: Start buying when the fear is highest.** The biggest fortunes are made here.

Depression (Severe Economic Collapse, -50% to -90%)

- Rare but devastating (e.g., **Great Depression, 1929**).
- Multi-year economic pain, mass unemployment, and financial system failures.
- Markets take **a decade or more to recover**.

✅ **Strategy:** Focus on cash, gold, real estate, and recession-proof businesses.

Tactical Patience: Knowing When to Strike

Most investors **struggle with timing** because emotions take over. But smart investors use **data, history, and patience** to wait for the best opportunities.

How to Apply Tactical Patience in Bear Markets:

📌 **Don't rush into a falling market.** Stocks can go lower than you expect.

📌 **Wait for true bargains.** Use historical valuations to see what's *really* undervalued.

📌 **Scale in gradually.** Buy in phases as the market bottoms, instead of all at once.

📌 **Ignore short-term noise.** Bull and bear markets both **take time to play out**.

My Opinion

From everything I've studied, **market cycles are predictable—but most investors ignore them.** They get greedy when prices are high and panic when prices are low. That's why they lose money.

In my opinion, the best investors **don't chase every opportunity**—they wait for the right moment. **They build cash reserves in bull markets, stay patient in downturns, and strike when others are fearful.**

Most people want **quick money**, but investing is a long game. If you **time your moves with the market cycle**, you don't need to take huge risks to get huge rewards. Bear markets don't last forever—**but if you're prepared, they can make you a fortune.**

In the next chapter, we'll break down **how to play defense in bear markets while positioning for big gains.**

CHAPTER 7: DEFENSIVE VS. OFFENSIVE STRATEGIES IN A DOWNTURN

"*The best offense is a good defense. But the best investors know when to switch between the two.*"

— Michael Fink

Why Strategy Matters More Than Ever in a Bear Market

When a bear market hits, most investors make **one of two mistakes**:

1 They panic and sell everything, locking in massive losses.

2 They "buy the dip" too early, getting wiped out as prices keep falling.

The truth is, **bear markets require a balance of both defensive and offensive strategies.** You need to **protect yourself from catastrophic losses** while also positioning for the **incredible buying opportunities that only happen once a decade.**

This chapter breaks down **when to play defense, when to go on offense, and how to rebalance your portfolio to survive and thrive in a downturn.**

How to Shield Your Portfolio from Catastrophic Losses

The first priority in a bear market is **not losing money.** Before thinking about gains, you must **protect your capital** and avoid the devastating losses that ruin investors.

Key Defensive Strategies in a Bear Market

✅ 1. Reduce Risky and Overvalued Assets

• Avoid **high-P/E stocks**, unprofitable companies, and speculative assets.

• Get out of **overhyped sectors** (crypto, meme stocks, over-leveraged tech companies).

✅ 2. Increase Cash Reserves

• Hold at least **20-30% of your portfolio in cash** to take advantage of opportunities.

• Use **short-term Treasury bonds** or **money market funds** for liquidity.

✅ 3. Own Defensive Stocks That Perform Well in Recessions

• **Consumer Staples:** People still buy food, soap, and household products (P&G, Coca-Cola).

- **Healthcare:** Medical companies and drug makers (Pfizer, Johnson & Johnson).

- **Utilities:** Electricity and water are always needed (Duke Energy, NextEra).

✅ 4. Limit Leverage and Debt

- **Pay down high-interest debt**—it becomes harder to manage in a downturn.

- Avoid margin trading—**markets can fall longer than you expect.**

✅ 5. Consider Hedging Strategies

- Buy **put options** on overvalued sectors to profit from declines.

- Hold **gold or silver** as a hedge against uncertainty.

- Use **inverse ETFs** (like SQQQ) to benefit from falling markets.

📌 **Goal: Don't let bear markets wipe you out. The biggest mistake is losing too much in the downturn, leaving you with no cash to buy when markets recover.**

When to Play Defense and When to Go All-In

The **biggest wealth transfers in history happen in recessions**—but only for those who know when to switch from **defense to offense**.

🗓 Phase 1: Early Bear Market – Play Defense

- **Sell overvalued assets, raise cash, and limit risk.**

- **Avoid "buying the dip" too early**—prices can keep falling.

- **Watch key economic indicators** (unemployment, corporate earnings).

Phase 2: Maximum Panic – Start Moving to Offense

- Stocks hit **historical valuation lows** (P/E ratios are cheap).

- **Investors are fearful**, and the media predicts economic doom.

- **Smart investors start buying undervalued assets cautiously.**

Phase 3: Early Recovery – Go All-In

- The Fed **stops raising rates** or **starts cutting them**.

- Unemployment **peaks and starts improving**.

- Big investors **start buying aggressively**—you should, too.

Key Rule: The best time to buy is **when it feels the hardest to do so.** When the media says, "It's different this time" and fear is everywhere, that's when fortunes are made.

Rebalancing for Bear Market Resilience
What is Portfolio Rebalancing?

Rebalancing is **adjusting your asset allocation** to maintain the right mix of stocks, bonds, cash, and other investments based on market conditions.

How to Rebalance in a Bear Market

1. Shift from Overvalued to Undervalued Assets

- Reduce **high-risk stocks** (tech, growth, speculative investments).

- Increase **defensive assets** (dividends, value stocks, gold, bonds).

📌 2. Increase Cash Holdings

- Bear markets **create amazing buying opportunities**, so keep dry powder ready.

- Sell **weak positions** before they lose more value.

📌 3. Rotate into Stronger Companies

- Recession-proof stocks like **consumer staples and healthcare** hold value.

- Quality companies **with low debt and strong cash flow** survive downturns.

📌 4. Dollar-Cost Average into Cheap Assets

- Instead of timing the exact bottom, **buy gradually as prices drop**.

- This lowers your average cost and reduces risk.

📌 5. Maintain Diversification

- **Don't put everything into one sector**—spread across stocks, bonds, real estate, and cash.

- **International markets** may recover faster than the U.S.

📌 6. Adjust as Market Conditions Change

- When **the economy starts improving**, move back into **growth stocks**.

- When **inflation drops**, interest-sensitive investments like **real estate** become attractive again.

📌 Goal: Rebalancing ensures you're protected in the downturn while preparing to take full advantage of the recovery.

My Opinion

After seeing multiple bear markets, **I've learned that being purely defensive or purely offensive is a mistake.** The best investors **adapt based on market conditions.**

Most people panic when the market crashes and **go 100% defensive**, missing out on huge opportunities. Others **go all-in too early**, thinking every dip is the bottom. Both approaches lose money.

In my opinion, **bear markets are about playing chess, not checkers.** You have to know **when to protect and when to strike**. If you can master that balance, **you'll not only survive downturns—you'll thrive in them.**

In the next chapter, we'll break down **how to read fear and greed in the market—and use it to your advantage.**

CHAPTER 8: THE ROLE OF FEAR AND GREED – SPOTTING MARKET SENTIMENT SHIFTS

"*Be fearful when others are greedy, and greedy when others are fearful.*"

— Warren Buffett

Why Market Sentiment Drives Prices More Than Fundamentals

Many people assume that **markets are logical**—that stock prices rise and fall based purely on earnings, economic data, and company performance.

That's a lie.

In reality, **fear and greed drive markets far more than fundamentals.** Stock prices don't just reflect numbers; they reflect **emotion**—investors' confidence, panic, euphoria, and despair.

The good news? **Investor sentiment is predictable.** By learning to **spot shifts in fear and greed**, you can:

✅ **Identify market tops before the crash.**

Bear Market Millionaire: 42 Bulletproof Strategies to Profit from ...

✅ **Buy near market bottoms when everyone else is panicking.**

✅ **Ignore media-driven hype and focus on reality.**

In this chapter, I'll break down **how to read investor sentiment, spot panic selling and euphoric buying, and use sentiment analysis to make smarter investment decisions.**

How to Recognize Panic Selling and Euphoric Buying

Investors swing between **two emotional extremes**:

🔥 FEAR (Bear Market Panic Selling)

• Market crashes **trigger extreme pessimism**.

• Investors **dump stocks** at any price just to "stop the bleeding."

• The media **predicts economic doom**, saying, *"This time is different."*

• Retail investors **abandon the market**, swearing never to invest again.

🚀 GREED (Bull Market Euphoria & Buying Frenzy)

• Stocks keep hitting **new highs** every week.

• The media **celebrates "unstoppable" markets**.

• Investors **ignore valuation metrics** and say, *"It'll keep going up forever."*

- Speculative assets **(crypto, meme stocks, NFTs)** skyrocket in price.

📌 **Rule of thumb:** *Markets peak when people think risk has disappeared. Markets bottom when people think investing is hopeless.*

Using Sentiment Analysis to Make Calculated Moves

Key Sentiment Indicators That Predict Market Moves

📉 1. The Fear & Greed Index

- Tracks **investor emotions on a scale of 0 (extreme fear) to 100 (extreme greed).**

- **Buy signals:** When the index is **below 20 (extreme fear)**—markets are oversold.

- **Sell signals:** When the index is **above 80 (extreme greed)**—markets are overbought.

📉 2. Put/Call Ratio (Investor Positioning Indicator)

- Measures the ratio of **put options (bearish bets) vs. call options (bullish bets).**

- High put/call ratios mean **investors are fearful** (buy signal).

- Low put/call ratios mean **investors are overly greedy** (sell signal).

📉 3. Volatility Index (VIX) – The Market's Fear Gauge

Bear Market Millionaire: 42 Bulletproof Strategies to Profit from ...

• High VIX (above 40) signals **panic and fear**—potential buying opportunities.

• Low VIX (below 15) signals **complacency**—markets are at risk of correction.

4. Media Headlines & Social Media Sentiment

• **Bullish headlines (euphoria)**: *"The Market Will Never Go Down Again!"* (Sell signal).

• **Bearish headlines (fear)**: *"Worst Crash Since 1929!"* (Buy signal).

5. Fund Flows (Where Money Is Moving)

• If money **flows into cash and bonds**, investors are fearful (buy stocks).

• If money **flows into speculative assets**, investors are greedy (reduce risk).

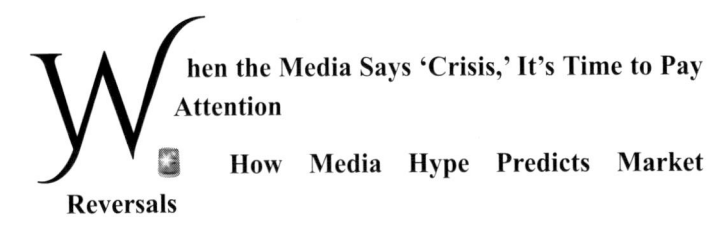

When the Media Says 'Crisis,' It's Time to Pay Attention

How Media Hype Predicts Market Reversals

During Market Crashes (Extreme Fear):

Headlines scream: *"Stocks Plunge! Investors in Full Panic!"*

The media **compares every crash to the Great Depression**.

📢 Experts say: *"This time is different. The market may never recover."*

This is usually the best time to buy.

During Market Bubbles (Extreme Greed):

📢 Headlines scream: *"Stocks Will Keep Rising Forever!"*

📢 New retail investors **jump into the market, believing it's easy money.**

📢 Experts say: *"This time is different. There's no risk anymore."*

This is usually the best time to sell.

📌 **Lesson:** *When the media fuels extreme fear, look for opportunities. When the media fuels extreme greed, start reducing risk.*

How to Profit from Market Sentiment Shifts

1. Buy When Fear Peaks

☑ When **everyone is selling in a panic**, look for **high-quality assets trading at discounts**.

☑ Ignore the noise and **trust historical data**—markets always recover.

2. Sell When Euphoria Peaks

☑ When **retail investors flood the market**, it's time to reduce risk.

- ✅ Start taking **profits in overvalued stocks and speculative assets**.

3. Use Sentiment Indicators to Time Entries and Exits

- ✅ When the **Fear & Greed Index is below 20**, start buying.
- ✅ When the **Fear & Greed Index is above 80**, start selling.

My Opinion

I've seen fear **wipe out** investors and greed **blind them to danger**. The people who make the most money **are the ones who stay calm when others panic and sell when others are greedy.**

In my opinion, **market sentiment is more powerful than fundamentals in the short term.** Fundamentals tell you what should happen, but sentiment tells you **what's happening right now.**

Most people **react to the news instead of anticipating it**. They wait until a market crash is **front-page news before they panic-sell**—which is exactly when they should be buying.

If you want to succeed, **train yourself to think the opposite of the crowd**. When fear dominates, **look for buying opportunities**. When greed dominates, **start preparing for a downturn.**

In the next chapter, we'll cover **how to find value in a bear market—and avoid falling into value traps.**

📌 SECTION III: STOCK MARKET STRATEGIES DURING A CRASH

CHAPTER 9: VALUE INVESTING IN A BEAR MARKET – FINDING UNDERVALUED GEMS

"Price is what you pay. Value is what you get."
— Warren Buffett

Why Bear Markets Are a Value Investor's Dream

When stocks are skyrocketing in a bull market, **everyone looks like a genius.** Even the worst companies see their share prices rise simply because there's too much easy money flowing into the system.

But when the bull run ends and the bear market takes over, **the hype disappears, and reality sets in.** Stocks that were propped up by speculation **crash back down to their true value**—and that's where the best investors strike.

Bear markets give value investors a once-in-a-decade opportunity to buy high-quality companies at deep discounts. The key is knowing **which stocks are true bargains and which ones are "value traps"** waiting to sink further.

In this chapter, we'll break down **how to find undervalued gems, avoid bad investments, and use proven value investing strategies to build wealth in bear markets.**

The Three Types of Undervalued Stocks in a Bear Market

1. Temporary Discounts (Market Overreactions)

• These are **high-quality companies** that temporarily drop due to panic selling.

• Their fundamentals **remain strong**, but investors overreact to bad news.

• **Example:** Amazon (AMZN) in 2008—fell to $35 per share but rebounded massively.

✅ **Best strategy: Look for strong companies with temporary price drops** and buy before they recover.

2. True Value Stocks (Hidden Gems)

• These companies are **fundamentally strong but overlooked**.

• They often have **low P/E ratios, high dividends, and consistent cash flow.**

• **Example:** McDonald's (MCD) in the 2008 crash—remained profitable while other stocks tanked.

✅ **Best strategy: Find recession-proof businesses that generate stable profits, even in downturns.**

3. Value Traps (Stocks That Look Cheap but Are Actually Dying)

• These stocks **seem undervalued** but have serious financial problems.

• They have **high debt, declining revenue, and outdated business models.**

• **Example:** Blockbuster (BBI) in the 2008 crash—looked cheap but was dying due to Netflix.

Warning: Avoid **companies that are cheap for a reason.** Always check their financials before buying.

How to Identify True Value in a Bear Market

1. Look at the Price-to-Earnings (P/E) Ratio

• Low P/E ratios can mean undervaluation, but **compare them to historical averages**.

• A P/E of **10 or lower** is typically considered cheap.

• Avoid companies with **suddenly rising P/E ratios**—this means their earnings are collapsing.

2. Check the Company's Balance Sheet

📌 **Strong Companies Have:**

✅ **Low debt** – High debt is dangerous in recessions.

✅ **High cash reserves** – Cash-rich companies survive bear markets.

✅ **Consistent profits** – Look for businesses that stayed profitable in past recessions.

🚩 **Red Flags:**

❌ High debt-to-equity ratios.

❌ Declining revenue for multiple years.

❌ Negative earnings for several quarters.

3. Focus on Companies with Economic Moats

A company with an **economic moat** has a competitive advantage that protects it from competition. These companies survive bear markets while weaker ones collapse.

Examples of strong moats:

✅ **Apple (AAPL)** – Strong brand and customer loyalty.

✅ **Coca-Cola (KO)** – Global dominance in beverages.

✅ **Visa (V)** – A monopoly on digital payments.

📌 **Rule of thumb:** *If a company can easily be replaced, it's not a good long-term investment.*

The Best Industries for Value Investing in a Bear Market

Certain sectors perform better than others in recessions. These are the industries **most likely to provide great value investing opportunities.**

1. Consumer Staples (Essential Goods & Services)

• People still **buy food, toiletries, and basic household items**, even in a recession.

- Best companies: **Procter & Gamble (PG), Unilever (UL), Coca-Cola (KO), PepsiCo (PEP).**

2. Healthcare (Recession-Proof Industry)

- People still **need medicine, doctor visits, and insurance**, even in bear markets.

- Best companies: **Pfizer (PFE), Johnson & Johnson (JNJ), UnitedHealth Group (UNH).**

3. Utilities (People Still Pay Their Electric Bills)

- No matter how bad the economy gets, **people need electricity, water, and gas.**

- Best companies: **Duke Energy (DUK), NextEra Energy (NEE), Dominion Energy (D).**

4. Dividend Stocks (Steady Cash Flow)

- Dividend-paying companies **reward investors even when stock prices drop.**

- Best companies: **3M (MMM), Verizon (VZ), ExxonMobil (XOM), Realty Income (O).**

🏹 **Lesson:** *In bear markets, focus on industries that keep making money even when people cut spending.*

Avoiding Value Traps – How to Spot Companies That Look Cheap but Are Actually Dying

🪨 **Red Flags That a Stock Is a Value Trap:**

❌ The stock price keeps falling with no signs of stabilization.

✘ The company has **declining revenue and growing debt.**

✘ The industry is shrinking due to disruption (think Blockbuster vs. Netflix).

✘ Insiders (CEOs, executives) are **selling their shares** instead of buying.

✘ The company relies on **high debt to survive**.

📌 **Example of a Value Trap:**

• **General Electric (GE)** – Once a strong company, but **declining revenue and excessive debt crushed its stock.**

✅ **How to Avoid Value Traps:**

• **Check earnings reports** – Is the company still making money?

• **Look at industry trends** – Is the company still competitive?

• **Watch insider buying** – If CEOs are selling, that's a bad sign.

My Opinion

I've seen investors **fall into two traps in bear markets**:

1️⃣ **They assume all cheap stocks are good deals.** (Some are cheap for a reason!)

2️⃣ **They avoid the market completely, missing out on true value.**

In my opinion, bear markets **are where the biggest wealth-building opportunities happen.** But you have to be **selective**. Just because a stock dropped 50% doesn't mean it's a bargain—it could still fall another 50%.

The best investors **look for quality, not just low prices.** If you find a **strong, cash-rich company trading at a discount, that's an opportunity you won't see again for years.**

In the next chapter, we'll explore **how dividend stocks can provide passive income during a bear market—and why they're one of the safest ways to invest in downturns.**

CHAPTER 10: DIVIDEND STOCKS – PASSIVE INCOME IN A RECESSION

"Do you know the only thing that gives me pleasure? It's to see my dividends coming in."

John D. Rockefeller

Why Dividend Stocks Outperform in Bear Markets

During a bear market, most investors focus on **how much their portfolio is shrinking**. But smart investors focus on **how much their portfolio is paying them.**

Dividend stocks are **one of the best ways to build wealth in downturns** because they provide **consistent cash flow** while markets are falling. Unlike growth stocks that depend on rising prices, dividend stocks **pay you regardless of market conditions**—making them a key part of any bear market strategy.

In this chapter, we'll cover:

- ✅ Why dividend stocks perform better in recessions.
- ✅ How to identify safe, high-yield dividend stocks.

✅ **How to reinvest dividends to maximize long-term growth.**

How Dividend Stocks Protect Your Wealth in a Bear Market

When markets crash, many investors panic because their portfolios are losing value. But **dividend investors don't care as much—because they're still getting paid.**

The Three Big Advantages of Dividend Stocks in Bear Markets

📌 1. Passive Income While Markets Are Down

- Even if stock prices drop, **dividends keep coming in.**

- You can **use dividend income to cover expenses** or reinvest it for compounding growth.

📌 2. Less Volatility Than Growth Stocks

- Dividend stocks tend to be **more stable** than speculative stocks.

- Investors **flock to dividend stocks in bear markets** for safety and income.

📌 3. Dividend Reinvestment (DRIP) Buys More Shares at Lower Prices

- Instead of withdrawing dividends, you can **reinvest them automatically.**

- During a downturn, reinvested dividends **buy more shares at cheaper prices.**

- This creates a **powerful compounding effect** when markets recover.

What Makes a Good Dividend Stock?

Not all dividend stocks are safe. Some companies **cut their dividends** in a recession, while others **increase their payouts every year**—even in downturns.

Key Metrics for Choosing Dividend Stocks

✅ 1. Dividend Yield (3-6% Is Ideal)

- **Yield = Annual Dividend ÷ Stock Price.**

- A 5% yield means you earn **$5 per year for every $100 invested.**

- Avoid stocks with **extremely high yields (10%+)**—they may be unsustainable.

✅ 2. Dividend Payout Ratio (Below 60% Is Best)

- **Payout Ratio = Dividend Paid ÷ Net Income.**

- A payout ratio above 80% means the company **is paying out too much** and may cut the dividend in a downturn.

✅ 3. Dividend Growth History

- Look for companies that **have increased dividends for 10+ years.**

- Companies with a strong history of raising dividends are **more likely to keep paying in bear markets.**

✅ 4. Strong Financials (Low Debt, High Cash Flow)

- Avoid companies with **high debt and weak earnings.**
- A strong balance sheet ensures **dividends will continue even in recessions.**

The Best Dividend Stocks for a Bear Market

Certain types of companies **consistently pay and grow dividends, even in recessions.** These are the safest places to put your money during a bear market.

1. Consumer Staples (Essential Goods People Always Buy)

- People still buy food, drinks, and household products in a recession.
- **Best picks: Procter & Gamble (PG), Coca-Cola (KO), PepsiCo (PEP), Unilever (UL)**

2. Utilities (Electricity, Water, and Gas Are Recession-Proof)

- People always pay their utility bills, making these stocks very stable.
- **Best picks: Duke Energy (DUK), NextEra Energy (NEE), Dominion Energy (D)**

3. Healthcare (People Always Need Medicine & Healthcare Services)

- Pharmaceuticals and insurance companies make money in any economy.

- **Best picks: Johnson & Johnson (JNJ), Pfizer (PFE), UnitedHealth Group (UNH)**

4. Dividend Aristocrats (Companies That Have Paid & Increased Dividends for 25+ Years)

- These stocks have survived **multiple recessions** and still increased dividends.

- **Best picks: 3M (MMM), McDonald's (MCD), Chevron (CVX), Realty Income (O)**

How to Build a Dividend Portfolio for Bear Market Income

If you want to **generate passive income in a bear market**, follow these steps:

📌 1. Buy Stocks with a History of Dividend Growth

- Look for companies that **increase dividends annually** (not just high yield).

📌 2. Diversify Across Multiple Dividend Sectors

- Own **consumer staples, utilities, healthcare, and dividend aristocrats** to stay balanced.

📌 3. Reinvest Dividends Automatically (DRIP Strategy)

- Instead of taking dividends as cash, **reinvest them to buy more shares.**

- Over time, this **compounds your returns massively.**

📌 4. Keep Some Cash to Buy More During Dips

• In a bear market, **buy dividend stocks on big drops to increase yield.**

📌 5. Don't Chase High Yields Without Checking Fundamentals

• Stocks with **unsustainable dividends** often collapse in bear markets.

• A stock with a **15% yield** is usually a warning sign—not an opportunity.

My Opinion

I've always believed **dividends are the most underrated wealth-building tool in investing.** Most people chase **hot growth stocks**, but the reality is, **steady dividend stocks quietly outperform over the long run.**

In my opinion, **bear markets expose weak companies and reward strong ones.** The companies that **continue paying dividends through a recession** prove that they are financially solid. Those that **cut dividends signal weakness.**

If you want **financial security in a downturn**, build a portfolio of **safe, dividend-paying stocks**. When the market crashes, **you'll still be getting paid.** And when it recovers, **you'll own even more shares from reinvesting dividends at low prices.**

In the next chapter, we'll cover **how to use short selling to profit from falling stocks**—for those who want to take an aggressive approach in a bear market.

CHAPTER 11: THE SHORT SELLING PLAYBOOK – PROFITING FROM FALLING STOCKS

"*The whole secret to winning in a bear market is to use the downtrend to your advantage.*"

— Michael Fink

How to Profit When Stocks Are Crashing

Most investors **only know how to make money when the market goes up.** But bear markets offer a unique opportunity: **you can profit as stocks fall**—if you know how.

Short selling is a strategy used by hedge funds, professional traders, and smart investors to **turn bear markets into major profit opportunities**. While risky, when done correctly, **short selling allows you to capitalize on overvalued stocks, collapsing companies, and failing industries.**

In this chapter, we'll break down:

✅ **How short selling works and when to use it.**

✅ **The risks and rewards of betting against the market.**

✅ **Proven strategies for short selling like a pro.**

What Is Short Selling?

Short selling is the opposite of buying stocks. Instead of **buying low and selling high**, you **sell high first, then buy low later to make a profit.**

How Short Selling Works (Step by Step):

📌 **Step 1:** Borrow shares from a broker at the current high price.

📌 **Step 2:** Sell those shares immediately on the market.

📌 **Step 3:** Wait for the stock price to drop.

📌 **Step 4:** Buy the shares back at the lower price.

📌 **Step 5:** Return the borrowed shares to your broker and keep the profit.

Example of a Short Sale:

• You believe **Company X is overvalued** at **$100 per share**.

• You **borrow 100 shares** from your broker and sell them, collecting **$10,000**.

• A month later, **Company X drops to $60 per share**.

• You **buy back the 100 shares** for **$6,000** and return them to your broker.

• **Your profit: $4,000** minus borrowing fees.

⚠️ **Warning:** If the stock goes **up** instead of down, your losses are unlimited—because there is no cap on how high a stock can go.

The Risks of Short Selling (Why Most Investors Avoid It)

While short selling can be profitable, **it carries major risks** that you must understand before attempting it.

1. Unlimited Losses

• When you **buy a stock**, the most you can lose is **100%** (if the stock goes to $0).

• When you **short a stock**, losses are **unlimited** because a stock can keep rising forever.

2. Short Squeezes (The Worst Nightmare for Short Sellers)

A **short squeeze** happens when a heavily shorted stock **suddenly surges higher**, forcing short sellers to **buy back shares at extreme losses.**

📌 Example: GameStop (GME) 2021 Short Squeeze

• Hedge funds heavily shorted GME, expecting it to crash.

• Retail traders **pushed the stock up from $10 to $400** in weeks.

• Shorts **lost billions** as they were forced to buy back at insane prices.

3. Borrowing Costs and Interest Fees

• Short selling requires **borrowing shares**, which means you **pay interest and fees** while holding the position.

- If the stock **doesn't drop fast enough**, these costs eat into your profits.

📌 **Lesson:** *Short selling can be extremely profitable, but the risks are much higher than simply buying stocks. Only use this strategy when you are confident a stock is overvalued and declining.*

The Best Strategies for Short Selling in a Bear Market

1. Shorting Overvalued Stocks (Bubble Stocks Ready to Burst)

- Look for stocks with **high P/E ratios, no earnings, and hype-driven prices.**

- Examples: Overhyped IPOs, speculative tech stocks, and meme stocks.

📌 **Best time to short:** When a stock is **overvalued, insiders are selling, and momentum is slowing down.**

2. Shorting Failing Businesses (Companies in Financial Trouble)

- Focus on companies with **high debt, declining revenue, and negative earnings.**

- Examples: **Blockbuster (BBI), Sears (SHLD), Lehman Brothers (LEH)** before they collapsed.

📌 **Best time to short:** When a company's **financials are getting worse, and its stock price has not yet collapsed.**

3. Shorting Market Indexes (When the Entire Market Is Dropping)

- Instead of shorting individual stocks, you can **short the entire market** using ETFs like:

◆ **SPY (S&P 500 ETF)** – Short when the S&P 500 is overvalued.

◆ **QQQ (Nasdaq ETF)** – Short when tech stocks are in a bubble.

📌 **Best time to short:** At the peak of a bull market, when the economy is showing signs of slowing down.

4. Buying Put Options (A Safer Alternative to Short Selling)

- Instead of shorting stocks, you can **buy put options**, which give you the right to sell a stock at a set price.

- This **limits your risk** while still allowing you to profit from falling stocks.

📌 **Best time to buy puts:** When a stock **shows clear signs of topping out** and **has weak financials.**

How to Manage Risk When Short Selling

📌 1. Never Short Without a Stop-Loss

- Set a **stop-loss** to exit the trade if the stock rises above a certain level.

- Example: If you short at **$100**, set a stop-loss at **$110** to limit losses.

📌 **2. Avoid Shorting Stocks with High Short Interest**

- If a stock has **too many short sellers**, it's at risk of a **short squeeze.**

📌 3. Use Small Positions & Diversify

- Never short **more than 5-10%** of your portfolio.

- Diversify across **multiple shorts** to spread risk.

📌 4. Be Ready to Cover Quickly

- **Short trades must be managed closely**—if a stock starts rebounding, exit immediately.

My Opinion

Short selling is **one of the riskiest ways to trade in a bear market**, but **it's also one of the most rewarding when done right.**

I've seen **short sellers make fortunes** betting against failing companies—but I've also seen **them get wiped out** when the market turned against them.

In my opinion, **most retail investors should avoid short selling individual stocks** because the risks are too high. Instead, I recommend:

✅ Using **put options** instead of shorting directly (limits risk).

✅ Shorting **overvalued index ETFs** instead of single stocks.

✅ Only shorting stocks **when fundamentals and sentiment align.**

If you **don't understand how short selling works,** stay

away. If you do, use it carefully as a **tactical tool**, not a main strategy.

In the next chapter, we'll cover **how to find defensive stocks that survive recessions—so you can balance your risk while markets crash.**

CHAPTER 12: DEFENSIVE SECTORS & "RECESSION-PROOF" STOCKS

"*When the economy tanks, the strong get stronger, and the weak disappear.*"
— Michael Fink

Why Defensive Stocks Matter in a Bear Market

When a bear market hits, most stocks **fall across the board**. But some companies **barely feel the impact**—or even perform better during economic downturns.

These **"recession-proof" stocks** belong to defensive sectors —industries that **provide essential goods and services** people continue buying no matter how bad the economy gets.

If you want to **protect your wealth and limit losses in a bear market**, defensive stocks are **the safest place to be**.

In this chapter, we'll cover:

✅ **The best defensive sectors for bear markets.**

✅ **Why some stocks outperform during recessions.**

✅ How to build a resilient portfolio using recession-proof stocks.

The Four Best Defensive Sectors for Bear Markets

1. Consumer Staples (People Still Buy Food & Household Products)

📌 Why It's Recession-Proof:

- No matter how bad the economy gets, **people still buy groceries, toothpaste, soap, and basic household goods.**

- These companies **have steady cash flow and strong pricing power.**

✅ Best Stocks in Consumer Staples:

- **Procter & Gamble (PG)** – Owns Tide, Gillette, Pampers, and more.

- **Coca-Cola (KO)** – Dominates the global beverage industry.

- **PepsiCo (PEP)** – Strong brand portfolio including Frito-Lay and Gatorade.

- **Unilever (UL)** – Owns Dove, Axe, Lipton, and Hellmann's.

📌 *Lesson: People cut back on vacations in a recession, but they don't stop brushing their teeth or drinking soda.*

2. Utilities (People Still Pay Their Electric Bills)

📌 Why It's Recession-Proof:

- Electricity, water, and natural gas **are essential services**—people **can't live without them.**

- Utility companies **have stable, regulated revenue streams.**

✅ **Best Stocks in Utilities:**

- **Duke Energy (DUK)** – One of the largest U.S. utility providers.

- **NextEra Energy (NEE)** – A leader in renewable energy and electric utilities.

- **Dominion Energy (D)** – A strong dividend-paying utility stock.

📌 **Lesson:** *People might cancel Netflix in a recession, but they won't stop paying their electricity bill.*

3. Healthcare (People Still Need Medicine & Medical Services)

📌 **Why It's Recession-Proof:**

- People **need healthcare regardless of the economy**—they can't delay surgeries, doctor visits, or medication.

- Healthcare companies **often receive government funding**, making them financially stable.

✅ **Best Stocks in Healthcare:**

- **Johnson & Johnson (JNJ)** – A diversified giant in pharmaceuticals, medical devices, and consumer health.

- **Pfizer (PFE)** – A leading drugmaker with strong revenue.

- **UnitedHealth Group (UNH)** – The largest health insurance provider in the U.S.

Bear Market Millionaire: 42 Bulletproof Strategies to Profit from ...

📌 **Lesson:** *People might delay buying a new iPhone, but they won't stop taking their life-saving medication.*

4. Discount Retailers (People Shop for Cheaper Goods in a Recession)

📌 **Why It's Recession-Proof:**

• When people **have less money, they switch from premium brands to discount stores.**

• **Low-cost retailers gain more customers** as people look for cheaper options.

✅ **Best Stocks in Discount Retail:**

• **Walmart (WMT)** – The largest discount retailer, thrives in recessions.

• **Costco (COST)** – Membership-based warehouse shopping keeps customers loyal.

• **Dollar General (DG)** – Gains market share as consumers trade down.

📌 **Lesson:** *In tough times, people stop shopping at high-end stores and start buying in bulk at Costco.*

How to Build a Defensive Portfolio for Recession Protection

To survive bear markets, **balance your portfolio with recession-proof stocks** while keeping cash ready for opportunities.

1. Hold 30-50% in Defensive Stocks

• Balance your portfolio with **consumer staples, utilities, healthcare, and discount retailers.**

2. Focus on Dividend Stocks for Passive Income

• Choose **companies that have a long history of paying and increasing dividends.**

• Dividend income **protects you while the market is down.**

3. Keep Some Cash for Buying Opportunities

• Even though defensive stocks hold up well, **bear markets create massive buying opportunities in other sectors.**

• Keep **10-30% of your portfolio in cash or short-term bonds** to buy assets at discounts.

4. Avoid High-Volatility Stocks in a Bear Market

• **Tech and speculative stocks** tend to fall the hardest in downturns.

• Shift out of **high-risk growth stocks** and into stable companies with consistent earnings.

📌 **Lesson:** *Bear markets wipe out overhyped stocks, but defensive stocks stay strong. Rotate into safer investments when a downturn begins.*

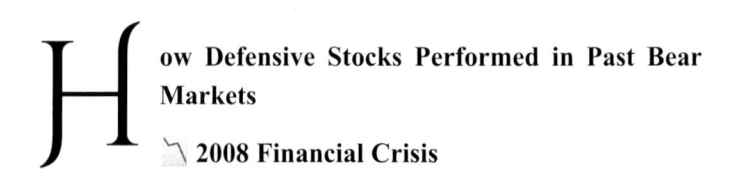

How Defensive Stocks Performed in Past Bear Markets

2008 Financial Crisis

- The S&P 500 dropped **-57%**, but consumer staples only fell **-22%.**

- **Walmart (WMT) stock actually rose** as more people shopped for cheaper goods.

📉 COVID-19 Crash (2020)

- Tech and travel stocks **crashed -40%+,** but healthcare stocks remained strong.

- **Johnson & Johnson (JNJ)** and **Pfizer (PFE)** outperformed the market.

📌 **Lesson:** *Recession-proof sectors don't just survive crashes—they often outperform the market.*

My Opinion

I've seen too many investors **go all-in on risky stocks, only to get wiped out in a bear market.** While high-growth stocks are exciting, **you need defensive stocks to survive downturns.**

In my opinion, **every investor should have at least 30% of their portfolio in recession-proof sectors.** These stocks don't just protect you when markets crash—they keep paying you through dividends, helping you grow wealth even in a downturn.

Bear markets don't last forever. **If you build a strong defensive portfolio now, you'll not only survive the next crash—you'll be in a position to take advantage of the recovery.**

In the next chapter, we'll explore **gold, silver, and commodi-**

ties—safe havens that often outperform when markets are in chaos.

📌 SECTION IV: ALTERNATIVE INVESTMENTS & HEDGING STRATEGIES

CHAPTER 13: GOLD, SILVER & COMMODITIES – SAFE HAVENS IN CHAOS

"*Gold is money. Everything else is credit.*"
— J.P. Morgan

Why Precious Metals Shine in Economic Uncertainty

When markets crash, investors panic. Stocks plummet, real estate freezes, and currencies can lose value. But throughout history, one asset has **held its worth through every crisis—gold.**

Precious metals like **gold and silver act as financial safe havens** during economic uncertainty. Unlike stocks, bonds, or cash, gold **doesn't rely on governments, corporations, or central banks** to maintain its value. That's why **gold prices typically rise when everything else is falling.**

In this chapter, we'll cover:

✅ Why gold and silver perform well in recessions.

✅ The right way to invest in precious metals.

✅ How commodities compare to cash in a bear market.

Why Gold & Silver Perform Well in Bear Markets

Precious metals have been used as **money and stores of value for over 5,000 years.** When confidence in financial systems drops, investors rush into gold and silver because:

📌 1. Gold & Silver Protect Against Inflation

• When central banks print money, inflation rises, and **fiat currencies lose purchasing power.**

• Gold historically **rises in price when inflation is high** because its supply is limited.

📌 2. Gold & Silver Hold Value in Market Crashes

• Stocks, bonds, and real estate **can collapse in a bear market**, but gold **typically rises or holds steady.**

• **Example:** During the 2008 crisis, the S&P 500 fell -57%, while gold **gained +24%.**

📌 3. Precious Metals Are a Hedge Against Currency Devaluation

• If a country's economy weakens, its **currency depreciates** —but gold remains valuable globally.

• **Example:** When the U.S. dollar weakens, gold prices tend to rise.

📌 4. Silver Has Industrial Demand, Adding Price Support

- Silver is used in **electronics, solar panels, and medical applications.**

- Even during recessions, industrial demand **helps keep silver prices stable.**

📌 **Lesson:** *Precious metals are financial insurance—they don't generate income, but they protect wealth during financial chaos.*

The Right Way to Invest in Gold and Silver

There are **multiple ways to own gold and silver**—some are safer, while others carry risks.

1. Physical Gold & Silver (Best for Long-Term Protection)

- **Gold bullion bars & coins** – Most secure but require storage.

- **Silver bullion** – Lower cost per ounce than gold, but bulkier.

- **Best coins:** American Eagles, Canadian Maple Leafs, Krugerrands.

✅ **Pros:**

- You own a real, tangible asset.

- No counterparty risk (not tied to a company or bank).

❌ **Cons:**

- Storage and security risks (need a safe or vault).

- Can be harder to sell quickly.

. . .

2. Gold & Silver ETFs (Best for Liquidity & Trading)

- **SPDR Gold Shares (GLD)** – Tracks gold prices.
- **iShares Silver Trust (SLV)** – Tracks silver prices.

✅ **Pros:**

- Easy to buy and sell like a stock.
- No storage concerns.

❌ **Cons:**

- You don't own **physical metal**—just a paper claim.
- Can be affected by financial system failures.

3. Gold & Silver Mining Stocks (Higher Risk, Higher Reward)

- Instead of owning gold itself, you invest in **gold mining companies**.
- **Best picks:** Barrick Gold (GOLD), Newmont (NEM), Wheaton Precious Metals (WPM).

✅ **Pros:**

- **Mining stocks can rise faster** than gold prices.
- Some pay **dividends**, unlike physical gold.

❌ **Cons:**

- **Mining companies can fail** even if gold prices rise.
- More volatile than owning physical gold.

4. Gold & Silver Futures & Options (For Experienced Traders Only)

- Futures allow you to **trade gold with leverage**, magnifying gains (or losses).

- **Very risky**—not recommended for long-term investors.

Commodities vs. Cash in Bear Markets

While cash **loses value to inflation**, commodities **hold their worth** because they are essential for global industries.

Best Commodities for a Bear Market

☑ 1. Oil & Energy (High Inflation Protection)

- Energy demand remains strong, even in recessions.

- **Best picks:** ExxonMobil (XOM), Chevron (CVX), Energy ETFs (XLE).

☑ 2. Agricultural Commodities (Food Prices Stay Strong)

- People still need wheat, corn, and soybeans.

- **Best picks:** Archer Daniels Midland (ADM), Deere & Co. (DE).

☑ 3. Industrial Metals (Infrastructure Demand Holds Up)

- Copper, aluminum, and steel remain valuable in construction and tech.

- **Best picks:** BHP Group (BHP), Freeport-McMoRan (FCX).

📌 *Lesson: Holding some commodities in a portfolio protects against inflation and economic uncertainty.*

How Much Gold & Silver Should You Own?

📌 **For Stability:** Hold **5-10% of your portfolio** in gold & silver.

📌 **For Inflation Protection:** Hold **10-20%** in precious metals & commodities.

📌 **For Extreme Crashes:** Some investors hold **30%+ in gold & silver** as financial insurance.

⚠️ **Warning:** Don't put 100% of your wealth into gold—**it doesn't generate income** like dividend stocks or real estate.

My Opinion

I've seen investors **completely ignore gold and silver**—until the economy crashes. Then, suddenly, **everyone wants it.** That's why I believe every investor should **own at least 5-10% of their portfolio in precious metals.**

Gold isn't meant to **make you rich**—it's meant to **protect your wealth when everything else is crashing.** It's like **an insurance policy** for your investments.

In my opinion, **physical gold and silver are the safest options**, while ETFs and mining stocks offer **more liquidity**

but carry some risk. Commodities are also smart investments, especially when inflation is rising.

If you want to **sleep better during a financial crisis**, having exposure to **gold, silver, and commodities** is one of the best ways to hedge against market chaos.

In the next chapter, we'll explore **bonds and fixed-income investments—another strategy for bear market protection and stability.**

CHAPTER 14: BONDS & FIXED INCOME FOR STABILITY

"In investing, what is comfortable is rarely profitable."
— Robert Arnott

Why Bonds Are a Safe Haven in Bear Markets

During stock market crashes, investors panic. They sell risky assets and look for **safety and stability**. This is where **bonds and fixed-income investments** come in.

Unlike stocks, bonds provide **steady interest payments** and are generally less volatile. In bear markets, when stocks are falling, high-quality bonds **often rise in value**—making them a critical part of a well-balanced portfolio.

In this chapter, we'll cover:

☑ **How bonds work and why they protect your portfolio.**

☑ **Which bonds perform best in a recession.**

☑ **How to balance bonds with stocks for bear market protection.**

. . .

How Bonds Work & Why They Perform Well in Downturns

A bond is essentially a **loan you give to a company, government, or organization** in exchange for interest payments.

📌 **Stocks vs. Bonds:**

- Stocks represent **ownership** in a company (higher risk, higher reward).

- Bonds represent **debt** (lower risk, fixed income).

When recessions hit, stocks **can lose 30-50% of their value**—but bonds **pay steady interest regardless of the market.**

📌 **Why Bonds Perform Well in Bear Markets:**

✅ **Low volatility** – Bonds don't swing wildly like stocks.

✅ **Guaranteed income** – You receive fixed interest payments.

✅ **Value increases when interest rates drop** – In recessions, central banks **cut interest rates**, making bonds more attractive.

📌 **Lesson:** *When stocks are collapsing, bonds provide stability and income.*

The Best Bonds for Bear Market Protection

Not all bonds are created equal. Some are **safe havens** in recessions, while others **carry risks similar to stocks.**

1. U.S. Treasury Bonds (The Safest Option)

• Backed by the U.S. government—virtually **risk-free**.

• Investors flock to Treasuries in market crashes, making them **highly liquid**.

• Interest rates **might be low, but safety is guaranteed**.

☑ **Best picks:**

• **T-Bills (Short-Term, 3-12 Months):** Great for parking cash.

• **10-Year Treasury Bonds:** Balance between safety and returns.

• **30-Year Treasury Bonds:** Best for long-term stability.

⚠ **Downside:** If inflation rises too fast, long-term Treasuries **lose value**.

2. Municipal Bonds (Tax-Free Income for Stability)

• Issued by **state and local governments**—often tax-free.

• Lower risk than corporate bonds, higher yield than Treasuries.

☑ **Best for:** High-income investors looking for **tax-free income**.

⚠ **Risk:** If the local economy crashes, some municipal bonds **may default**.

. . .

3. Investment-Grade Corporate Bonds (Higher Yield, Still Safe)

• Issued by **strong, financially stable companies** (Apple, Microsoft).

• **Higher interest rates than government bonds**, but riskier.

✅ **Best picks:**

• **AAA-rated corporate bonds** – The safest corporate debt.

• **Short-term corporate bonds (1-5 years)** – Less risk than long-term bonds.

🪦 Risk: If a company **goes bankrupt, bondholders could lose money.**

4. High-Yield (Junk) Bonds – Big Risk, Big Reward

• Issued by **weaker companies** with higher default risks.

• High interest rates **(6-12%+), but at the cost of higher risk.**

✅ **Best for:** High-risk investors willing to gamble in bear markets.

🪦 **Warning:** Junk bonds are **not safe havens**—they act more like stocks in downturns.

. . .

Bonds vs. Stocks: How to Balance for a Bear Market

📌 **Traditional Portfolio Allocation (60/40 Strategy):**

◆ **60% Stocks + 40% Bonds** – Provides **growth + downside protection**.

📌 **More Conservative Bear Market Allocation:**

◆ **40% Stocks + 50% Bonds + 10% Cash** – Greater safety, lower risk.

📌 **Extreme Recession Hedge:**

◆ **20% Stocks + 60% Bonds + 20% Gold/Silver** – Maximum protection.

📌 **Lesson:** *The older you are, the more bonds you should own. If you're young, you can take more stock market risk.*

Bond ETFs: The Easy Way to Invest in Bonds

If you don't want to buy individual bonds, you can invest in **bond ETFs**, which provide diversification.

📌 **Best Bond ETFs for Stability:**

✅ **BND (Total Bond Market ETF)** – Holds a mix of Treasuries and corporate bonds.

✅ **TLT (Long-Term Treasury ETF)** – Good for hedging against stock market declines.

✅ **LQD (Investment-Grade Corporate Bonds)** – Higher yield, but still safe.

⚠️ **Warning:** Long-term bond ETFs **fall when interest rates rise.**

When to Buy & Sell Bonds in a Bear Market

📌 **Best Time to Buy Bonds:**

✅ When interest rates are **high** (before the Fed starts cutting rates).

✅ When recession risks are rising.

📌 **Best Time to Sell Bonds:**

❌ When inflation is **rising fast** (bonds lose value in inflationary environments).

❌ When the Fed **signals interest rate hikes** (makes bonds less attractive).

📌 *Lesson: Buy bonds when the Fed is cutting rates. Sell when inflation is climbing fast.*

How Much of Your Portfolio Should Be in Bonds?

📌 **For Aggressive Investors:** 10-20% in bonds (higher stock exposure).

📌 **For Moderate Investors:** 30-50% in bonds (balanced risk).

📌 **For Conservative Investors:** 60-80% in bonds (maximum safety).

⬛ **Warning:** Don't put 100% in bonds—over time, stocks provide better long-term growth.

My Opinion

I've seen bear markets **destroy portfolios that were too aggressive**—but I've also seen investors **play too safe and miss growth opportunities.**

In my opinion, **bonds are essential for bear market protection, but they shouldn't be your entire portfolio.** They provide **stability, cash flow, and safety when stocks crash** —but you still need **stocks, commodities, and real assets for long-term growth.**

If you're **worried about a recession, increasing your bond exposure is smart.** But don't go all-in—**having some risk exposure ensures you benefit from the recovery when the bear market ends.**

In the next chapter, we'll explore **how crypto performs in bear markets—and whether Bitcoin is really "digital gold."**

CHAPTER 15: CRYPTO IN A BEAR MARKET – OPPORTUNITY OR TRAP?

"*Bitcoin is a technological tour de force."*
— Bill Gates

Is Crypto a Safe Haven or Just Another Risky Asset?

Cryptocurrency has exploded in popularity over the past decade. Bitcoin, Ethereum, and other digital assets have been called **"the future of money"** and **"digital gold."** But when bear markets hit, does crypto truly offer a safe haven—or is it just another volatile asset that crashes alongside stocks?

In this chapter, we'll explore:

✅ **How crypto performs in bear markets.**

✅ **Whether Bitcoin is really "digital gold."**

✅ **Which cryptos have long-term potential vs. which ones are hype.**

. . .

How Crypto Has Performed in Past Bear Markets

📉 2018 Crypto Crash (Bitcoin Fell -85%)

- After the 2017 Bitcoin boom, **BTC crashed from $20,000 to $3,200** in one year.

- Thousands of **altcoins disappeared**—only the strongest projects survived.

📉 2022 Crypto Winter (Bitcoin Dropped -75%)

- **Bitcoin crashed from $69,000 to $16,000** following the stock market downturn.

- Major crypto platforms **(Terra/Luna, Celsius, FTX)** collapsed.

📌 **Lesson:** *Crypto tends to crash hard in bear markets—unlike gold, which holds value better.*

Is Bitcoin Really "Digital Gold"?

📌 Similarities Between Bitcoin & Gold:

✅ **Limited supply** – Bitcoin has a fixed cap of **21 million coins**, like gold's scarcity.

✅ **Decentralized** – No government or central bank controls Bitcoin.

✅ **Seen as an inflation hedge** – Some investors use Bitcoin to protect against fiat currency devaluation.

📌 Key Differences Between Bitcoin & Gold:

✘ **Bitcoin is highly volatile** – It can drop **50-80% in a bear market.**

✘ **Gold has a 5,000-year history as money** – Bitcoin is only a decade old.

✘ **Regulatory risks** – Governments could ban or restrict Bitcoin use.

🔖 **Lesson:** *Bitcoin may be a long-term store of value, but it is not yet as stable as gold.*

The Cryptos Most Likely to Survive a Bear Market

Not all cryptos will survive a recession. In every bear market, **weak projects disappear, and only the strongest survive.**

1. Bitcoin (BTC) – The King of Crypto

• The **most decentralized, most secure** digital asset.

• Large institutions and hedge funds now hold Bitcoin.

• Historically, **Bitcoin crashes in bear markets but recovers stronger.**

2. Ethereum (ETH) – The Smart Contract Leader

• **Ethereum powers decentralized apps (DeFi, NFTs, Web3).**

• Upgraded to **Ethereum 2.0** for faster and cheaper transactions.

• Unlike Bitcoin, Ethereum **generates revenue through smart contracts.**

3. Stablecoins (USDT, USDC) – Safe Havens in Crypto

• Pegged to **$1 USD**, offering a cash-like safe haven.

• Used for trading, but **not an investment for long-term growth.**

📊 **Cryptos to Avoid in a Bear Market:**

❌ **Overhyped Meme Coins** (Doge, Shiba Inu) – No real use case.

❌ **Scam Projects & Ponzi Schemes** – Many cryptos fail during downturns.

❌ **New "Hype" Altcoins** – Most collapse when the bull run ends.

📌 **Lesson:** *Stick to Bitcoin, Ethereum, and stablecoins in bear markets—avoid speculative altcoins.*

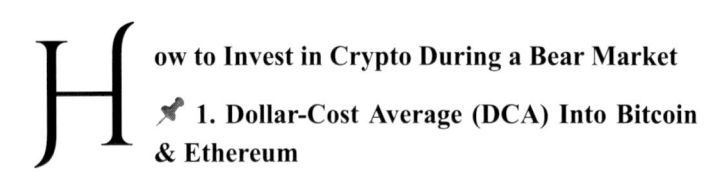

How to Invest in Crypto During a Bear Market

📌 **1. Dollar-Cost Average (DCA) Into Bitcoin & Ethereum**

• Instead of buying all at once, **invest small amounts over time**.

• Reduces risk if prices keep falling.

📌 **2. Hold Stablecoins to Buy Crypto at the Bottom**

• **Keep USDC or USDT on hand** to buy Bitcoin when prices crash.

- Avoid keeping too much in exchanges—some may fail in a crisis.

📌 3. Only Invest What You Can Afford to Lose

- Crypto can **drop 50-80% in a bear market**—never bet your life savings.

📌 4. Avoid High-Leverage Crypto Trading

- Many investors **got wiped out using leverage in past crashes.**

- Play it safe—**crypto is risky enough without leverage.**

📌 5. Secure Your Crypto in Cold Storage

- **Use a hardware wallet (Ledger, Trezor)** to store Bitcoin safely.

- **Don't leave funds on exchanges**—they can collapse (like FTX).

📌 **Lesson:** *Bear markets shake out weak hands. The smartest crypto investors buy Bitcoin and Ethereum when fear is at its highest.*

Will Crypto Survive Future Recessions?

📌 Bull Case for Crypto:

✅ Bitcoin's adoption is growing—**big institutions now hold BTC.**

✅ Ethereum powers DeFi, NFTs, and smart contracts—**real-world use cases.**

✅ Governments **can't print Bitcoin**, making it attractive in inflationary times.

📌 **Bear Case for Crypto:**

❌ Crypto remains highly volatile—**not a true safe haven yet.**

❌ Governments could **regulate or ban crypto** in the future.

❌ Many **altcoins will disappear**—only the strongest will survive.

My Opinion

I've seen too many investors **treat crypto like a lottery ticket**—going all in on meme coins and hype projects, only to lose everything in a bear market.

In my opinion, **Bitcoin and Ethereum have long-term value**—but you need patience. Bear markets **wipe out weak hands and bad projects**, but they also provide **amazing buying opportunities** for serious investors.

If you want to invest in crypto during a bear market:

✅ Stick to **Bitcoin & Ethereum**—they have the best survival chances.

✅ **Don't use leverage**—crypto is risky enough without it.

✅ **Store your crypto securely**—don't trust exchanges blindly.

✅ **Only invest money you can afford to lose**—crypto remains a high-risk asset.

Bear Market Millionaire: 42 Bulletproof Strategies to Profit from …

In the next chapter, we'll explore **options trading—how to hedge risk and profit from market downturns using put options.**

CHAPTER 16: OPTIONS TRADING FOR DOWNTURNS – HEDGING & SPECULATING

"*The stock market is filled with individuals who know the price of everything but the value of nothing.*"

— Philip Fisher

How Options Can Protect You in a Bear Market

Bear markets bring chaos—stocks crash, portfolios shrink, and fear takes over. But what if you could **make money while markets fall** instead of just watching your investments bleed?

That's where **options trading comes in.**

Options allow you to:

✅ **Hedge your portfolio** – Protect your stocks from falling prices.

✅ **Profit from market downturns** – Make money when stocks drop.

Bear Market Millionaire: 42 Bulletproof Strategies to Profit from ...

✅ **Reduce risk while increasing returns** – Use less capital to control more assets.

While options **can be complex and risky**, learning the right strategies can **turn a bear market into a massive opportunity.**

In this chapter, we'll break down:

✅ **How put options work to profit from falling stocks.**

✅ **The best options strategies for bear markets.**

✅ **How to hedge your portfolio and limit downside risk.**

Understanding Put Options – The Key to Profiting in Bear Markets

A **put option** is a contract that gives you the **right (but not the obligation) to sell a stock at a set price before a certain date.**

How Put Options Work (Step by Step):

📌 **Step 1:** You buy a put option on Stock XYZ with a **strike price of $100**.

📌 **Step 2:** If the stock **drops to $80**, you can still sell it for **$100**, making a profit.

📌 **Step 3:** If the stock **rises instead**, you can let the option expire, losing only the small amount you paid (the premium).

✅ **Why Puts Are Powerful in Bear Markets:**

- You **profit when stocks go down**—no need to own the stock.

- Limited risk—**the most you can lose is the premium you paid.**
- Can be used for **hedging or speculation.**

📌 **Lesson:** *Buying puts is like buying "insurance" on your portfolio—when markets crash, your puts increase in value.*

The Best Options Strategies for Bear Markets

1. Buying Put Options (Simple & Effective for Profiting in Downturns)

- If you think a stock **will drop**, buy a put option.
- Example: Buy a **put on Tesla (TSLA) if you expect a big drop.**
- Works well when **volatility is rising** and markets are crashing.

🟫 **Risk:** If the stock **doesn't drop in time**, the option expires worthless.

2. Protective Puts (Hedging Your Portfolio Without Selling Stocks)

- If you own stocks **but don't want to sell**, buy puts to protect them.
- Example: If you own **100 shares of Apple (AAPL) at $150**, buy a put at **$140** to limit losses.
- Works well when you expect **short-term volatility** but want to stay invested.

Bear Market Millionaire: 42 Bulletproof Strategies to Profit from …

⬛ **Risk:** Buying puts **costs money (premium),** so if stocks don't fall, you lose the premium.

3. Covered Calls (Generating Income While Holding Stocks)

• If markets are **flat or slightly bearish**, sell call options against stocks you own.

• Example: Own **100 shares of Microsoft (MSFT)? Sell a call at $250** to collect income.

• If the stock **stays below $250**, you **keep the premium as profit.**

⬛ **Risk:** If the stock **rises too much**, you miss out on gains.

4. Cash-Secured Puts (Buying Stocks at a Discount)

• If you want to buy a stock **at a lower price**, sell a put option.

• Example: Sell a **put on Amazon (AMZN) at $80**—if the stock drops, you buy it at a discount.

• Works well when markets **are down, but you want to buy quality stocks cheap.**

⬛ **Risk:** If the stock **doesn't drop, you don't get to buy it —but you keep the premium as income.**

. . .

How to Use Options to Hedge Your Portfolio

1. Use Put Options as Insurance

- Buy puts on stocks **you own to limit losses in a crash.**
- Example: Own **S&P 500 ETF (SPY)? Buy a SPY put to protect against a bear market.**

2. Hedge Using Inverse ETFs

- Instead of shorting, buy **put options on the S&P 500 (SPY) or Nasdaq (QQQ).**
- Works well in **high-volatility markets when you expect a downturn.**

3. Use Spreads to Reduce Risk

- A **bear put spread** (buy one put, sell another) **reduces cost and risk.**
- Works well in **moderate downturns when you want limited downside exposure.**

📌 **Lesson:** *If you don't want to sell stocks in a bear market, options provide protection while keeping you invested.*

When to Use Options in a Bear Market

📌 **Best Times to Buy Put Options:**

☑ **Before earnings reports** (for weak companies likely to drop).

☑ **When volatility is rising** (fear is taking over).

☑ **When a stock is overvalued** (has risen too fast with weak fundamentals).

📌 **Best Times to Sell Covered Calls:**

☑ **When the market is moving sideways** (not crashing, just weak).

☑ **On stocks you don't plan to sell** but want extra income.

📌 **Best Times to Sell Cash-Secured Puts:**

☑ **When you want to buy a stock at a lower price.**

☑ **When the market is down, but you expect a rebound.**

The Risks of Options Trading (What Most People Get Wrong)

1. Options Expire Worthless If You Time the Market Wrong

• If the stock **doesn't move in your favor before expiration, you lose the premium paid.**

2. Volatility Crush Can Wipe Out Gains

• If you buy puts **when volatility is high, you may lose money even if stocks drop.**

3. Selling Naked Options Can Lead to Unlimited Losses

• If you sell options **without owning the stock or having cash to cover it**, your losses can be **massive.**

📌 *Lesson: Options trading can be extremely profitable, but only if you understand risk management.*

My Opinion

I've seen options **make and break traders** during bear markets. While options are **incredibly powerful**, most people **use them the wrong way.**

In my opinion, the best **bear market options strategies are simple:**

☑ **Buy put options on weak stocks** to profit from downturns.

☑ **Use protective puts** if you own stocks but want downside protection.

☑ **Sell cash-secured puts** to buy quality stocks at a discount.

If you don't understand options, **start small and avoid high-risk strategies.** Used wisely, options **can be a game-changer in bear markets**—but reckless trading can wipe out your portfolio.

In the next chapter, we'll cover **how real estate investing works in a bear market—and why recessions can create once-in-a-lifetime deals.**

📌 SECTION V: REAL ESTATE & BUSINESS STRATEGIES IN ECONOMIC CHAOS

CHAPTER 17: BUYING REAL ESTATE AT RECESSION DISCOUNTS

"Be fearful when others are greedy, and greedy when others are fearful."

— Warren Buffett

Why Bear Markets Are the Best Time to Buy Real Estate

During economic booms, **real estate prices skyrocket**—bidding wars, overleveraged buyers, and speculation drive prices beyond fundamentals. But when recessions hit, things change.

Suddenly, properties **sit on the market longer**, sellers become desperate, and **massive discounts appear** for buyers who have cash or financing ready.

Recessions create **some of the best real estate buying opportunities in decades.** The key is knowing:

✅ **Where to find the best deals.**

✅ **How to buy undervalued properties safely.**

✅ **How to profit when the market recovers.**

In this chapter, we'll break down:

✅ **Why real estate crashes in bear markets.**

✅ **How to identify the best recession-proof properties.**

✅ **The best financing strategies for buying in a downturn.**

Why Real Estate Prices Drop in a Bear Market

📉 1. Rising Interest Rates Make Homes Less Affordable

- The **Federal Reserve raises rates to fight inflation**, increasing mortgage costs.
- As borrowing gets expensive, **buyers disappear** and home prices fall.

📉 2. Mass Layoffs Lead to Foreclosures

- Job losses mean **homeowners can't make mortgage payments.**
- Banks **foreclose on properties, flooding the market with cheap homes.**

📉 3. Fear Keeps Buyers on the Sidelines

- Most people believe, **"Real estate is a bad investment in a recession."**
- This fear **creates opportunities for smart investors.**

📌 **Lesson:** *Recessions push weak hands out of the market—this is where fortunes are made.*

. . .

Where to Find the Best Real Estate Deals in a Recession

1. Foreclosures & Bank-Owned Properties (REOs)

• Homes that have **gone through foreclosure and are now owned by banks.**

• Banks **sell them at deep discounts** to get them off their books.

☑ How to Find Them:

• Check **HUD Homes** (government foreclosures).

• Look at **bank-owned property listings.**

• Work with **agents who specialize in distressed properties.**

Risk: Some foreclosed homes **need major repairs—inspect before buying.**

2. Short Sales (Pre-Foreclosures)

• When homeowners **owe more than their home is worth**, they may sell **for less than the mortgage balance.**

• Banks **approve these sales to avoid full foreclosure.**

☑ How to Find Them:

• Look for **"Short Sale" listings** on real estate websites.

• Contact **distressed homeowners directly** before foreclosure.

⬛ **Risk: Takes longer** than regular home purchases due to bank approval.

3. Motivated Sellers (People Who Need to Sell Fast)

• In a recession, **some homeowners MUST sell**—job loss, relocation, divorce, financial distress.

• These sellers **are willing to negotiate below market value.**

☑ **How to Find Them:**

• Look for listings **priced below market value.**

• Use **"We Buy Houses" marketing to attract distressed sellers.**

• Search for **expired listings where sellers failed to sell.**

⬛ **Risk:** Some sellers **may still be emotionally attached** and reject low offers.

4. Commercial Real Estate Distress (Multi-Family & Retail)

• **Office spaces, hotels, and retail buildings** suffer the most in recessions.

• Investors who overpaid **may be forced to sell at huge discounts.**

☑ **Best Deals:**

• **Multi-family apartment buildings** – Rents stay stable in downturns.

- **Retail & office spaces in good locations** – Long-term opportunities when the economy recovers.

⚠️ Risk: Commercial properties take longer to recover than residential real estate.

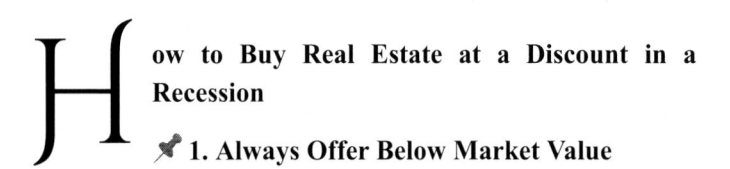

How to Buy Real Estate at a Discount in a Recession

📌 1. Always Offer Below Market Value

- **Start at 20-30% below asking price**—many sellers will negotiate.

📌 2. Look for Seller Financing Deals

- Some owners will **finance the sale themselves** to attract buyers.
- **Low or no down payment** options may be available.

📌 3. Use Cash or Hard Money to Close Faster

- **Cash buyers get better deals** in a slow market.
- Hard money lenders offer **fast loans**, but with **higher interest rates.**

📌 4. Buy Properties That Generate Cash Flow Immediately

- Don't rely on price appreciation—**buy rental properties that make money NOW.**

📌 5. Consider House Hacking

- Live in one unit, rent the rest—**lowers your housing costs while building equity.**

The Best Financing Strategies for Buying in a Downturn

📌 **1. Conventional Loans (Best for Primary Residences)**

- Fixed-rate loans offer **stable payments even in recessions.**

- **Best for:** Long-term buyers who want **low-interest financing.**

📌 **2. FHA Loans (Low Down Payment, Great for First-Time Buyers)**

- Requires **only 3.5% down.**

- **Best for:** House hacking (buying multi-family properties).

📌 **3. Hard Money Loans (Fastest Way to Buy Discounted Deals)**

- **Best for:** Investors flipping or buying distressed properties.

- High interest rates but **quick access to cash.**

📌 **4. Seller Financing (Best for Deals with No Banks Involved)**

- The seller acts as the lender—**great in high-interest environments.**

- **Best for:** Buyers who **can't get traditional bank loans.**

📌 *Lesson: Use financing strategically to buy deals before the market recovers.*

How to Profit When the Market Recovers

📌 1. Buy in a Recession, Sell in a Boom

• The best time to **buy real estate is when no one wants it.**

• The best time to **sell is when everyone is trying to buy.**

📌 2. Rent Properties for Cash Flow While Waiting for Price Recovery

• Don't wait for appreciation—**make money through rent while holding.**

📌 3. Refinance When Interest Rates Drop

• Buy properties when rates are **high and prices are low.**

• Refinance **later when rates drop, increasing cash flow.**

📌 4. Add Value to Distressed Properties

• **Renovate & force appreciation**—buy cheap, fix up, sell higher.

• **Convert single-family homes into multi-unit rentals.**

📌 5. Sell to Institutional Investors in the Next Boom

• Big funds **buy real estate aggressively** when markets recover.

• **Hold until institutions start buying again**, then sell at a premium.

My Opinion

I've seen bear markets **wipe out overleveraged investors**—but I've also seen **smart buyers make fortunes** by purchasing real estate at rock-bottom prices.

In my opinion, **real estate is one of the best investments during a recession**—but only if you buy **cash-flowing properties and avoid speculation**.

✅ **Best strategy:** Buy distressed properties **20-30% below market value** and hold for cash flow.

❌ **Biggest mistake:** Buying **overpriced properties and hoping they appreciate.**

If you're prepared, **a real estate crash isn't a disaster—it's a once-in-a-lifetime buying opportunity.**

In the next chapter, we'll cover **how to invest in REITs (real estate investment trusts) as a hands-off way to profit from downturns.**

CHAPTER 18: INVESTING IN REITS – A PASSIVE APPROACH TO BEAR MARKET REAL ESTATE

"Owning real estate is great. But what if you could own property without the headaches?"

— Michael Fink

Why REITs Are the Easiest Way to Invest in Real Estate

Real estate is one of the best asset classes for building wealth—but owning physical property **requires time, effort, and capital**. If you want exposure to real estate **without managing tenants, fixing toilets, or dealing with financing**, Real Estate Investment Trusts (REITs) offer a powerful alternative.

REITs allow investors to **own income-producing real estate without buying properties directly**. They trade like stocks, **pay high dividends**, and historically **perform well during economic recoveries**.

In this chapter, we'll cover:

✅ **How REITs work and why they are great in bear markets.**

☑ The best types of REITs for recession investing.

☑ How to build a REIT portfolio for long-term wealth.

How REITs Work & Why They're Attractive in Bear Markets

A **Real Estate Investment Trust (REIT)** is a company that owns and manages income-producing real estate. Investors **buy shares in the REIT**, which owns properties like:

- Office buildings
- Shopping malls
- Apartments
- Warehouses & storage facilities
- Healthcare facilities

REITs generate **rental income from tenants** and **pay out 90%+ of their profits as dividends** to investors.

📌 **Why REITs Are Good in a Bear Market:**

☑ **High Dividend Yields** – Most REITs pay **4-8% annually**, providing cash flow.

☑ **Hedge Against Inflation** – Rents rise with inflation, increasing REIT income.

☑ **Own Real Estate Without Management Hassles** – No tenants, no property maintenance.

📌 **Lesson:** *If you want passive income from real estate without owning properties, REITs are the best solution.*

The Best Types of REITs for Bear Market Investing

Not all REITs perform equally in a downturn. Some sectors get crushed, while others thrive.

1. Residential REITs (Best for Recession-Proof Housing)

• Owns **apartment buildings and rental communities**.

• People **always need housing**, making it a stable investment.

• **Best picks:** AvalonBay Communities (AVB), Equity Residential (EQR).

✅ **Why Invest? Rental demand stays strong in recessions.**

🚫 **Avoid:** Luxury apartment REITs—renters downgrade in bear markets.

2. Healthcare REITs (Recession-Proof Medical Facilities)

• Owns **hospitals, nursing homes, and medical office buildings**.

• Healthcare demand **doesn't drop in recessions**.

• **Best picks:** Welltower (WELL), Ventas (VTR), Omega Healthcare (OHI).

✅ **Why Invest? Medical services remain essential no matter the economy.**

- **Risk:** Government regulation can affect healthcare REIT profits.

3. Industrial REITs (Warehouses & Logistics Centers)

• Owns **storage facilities, distribution centers, and fulfillment warehouses**.

• **E-commerce boom** keeps demand for warehouses high.

• **Best picks:** Prologis (PLD), Duke Realty (DRE).

- **Why Invest? Amazon, Walmart, and Shopify all rely on warehouse space.**

- **Risk:** If the economy crashes, shipping demand may decline.

4. Retail REITs (Only Buy Essential Shopping Centers)

• Owns **shopping malls and retail spaces**.

• **Discount stores & grocery-anchored centers** do well in recessions.

• **Best picks:** Realty Income (O), Simon Property Group (SPG).

- **Why Invest? People still shop at Walmart, Costco, and grocery stores in downturns.**

- **Avoid:** High-end malls and department store REITs—these struggle in recessions.

. . .

REITs vs. Owning Physical Property – Which Is Better?

Feature

REITs

Physical Real Estate

Ease of Investment

Buy shares like stocks

Requires finding & financing properties

Liquidity

Sell anytime

Hard to sell quickly

Passive Income

Dividend payouts monthly/quarterly

Rental income (if tenants pay)

Management Effort

No effort needed

Landlord responsibilities

Leverage

No leverage (cash only)

Can use mortgages for leverage

Risk in a Recession

Some REITs may decline, but diversified

Individual properties may lose value

📌 **Lesson:** *REITs are best for passive investors. Owning property is better for hands-on investors who want more control.*

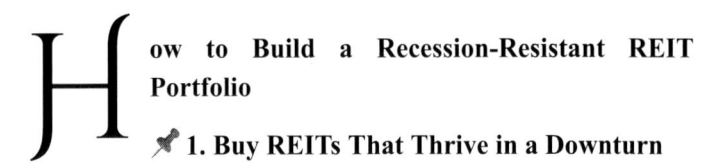

How to Build a Recession-Resistant REIT Portfolio

📌 1. Buy REITs That Thrive in a Downturn

✅ Focus on **residential, healthcare, and industrial REITs** (people always need housing, medical care, and logistics).

📌 2. Diversify Across Multiple REIT Sectors

✅ Don't put all money in one type of REIT—own different categories for balance.

📌 3. Prioritize High-Dividend REITs for Passive Income

✅ Look for **REITs with a history of paying and increasing dividends.**

📌 4. Use REIT ETFs for Broad Diversification

✅ If you don't want to pick individual REITs, use REIT ETFs like:

• **VNQ (Vanguard Real Estate ETF)** – Broad REIT market exposure.

• **SCHH (Schwab U.S. REIT ETF)** – Low-cost REIT index fund.

📌 5. Buy REITs During Market Panics & Sell in Booms

Bear Market Millionaire: 42 Bulletproof Strategies to Profit from ...

✅ **REITs often get oversold in bear markets**, creating cheap entry points.

When to Buy & Sell REITs in a Bear Market

📌 **Best Time to Buy REITs:**

✅ When **interest rates are peaking** (high rates lower REIT prices).

✅ When **real estate panic is high**, but fundamentals are strong.

✅ When **REIT dividend yields are at historically high levels**.

📌 **Best Time to Sell REITs:**

❌ When **the economy is overheating** and real estate prices are too high.

❌ When **interest rates are expected to rise sharply** (makes financing real estate more expensive).

❌ When **dividends get cut**, signaling financial trouble in the REIT.

📌 **Lesson:** *Buy REITs when fear is high. Sell them when greed is taking over.*

My Opinion

I've seen real estate cycles repeat **over and over again**—and every time, **REITs get sold off too**

aggressively in bear markets. When that happens, **it's a great buying opportunity.**

In my opinion, **owning a mix of physical real estate and REITs is the best strategy.** REITs provide **passive income and diversification**, while physical properties give you **more control over assets and leverage.**

If you're looking for a **hands-off way to invest in real estate during a recession**, REITs are an **excellent choice**—especially if you focus on **recession-proof sectors.**

In the next chapter, we'll cover **how to prepare mentally and emotionally for bear markets—because surviving downturns isn't just about strategy, it's about mindset.**

CHAPTER 19: MASTERING THE BEAR MARKET MINDSET – HOW TO STAY RATIONAL WHEN OTHERS PANIC

"*The stock market is a device for transferring money from the impatient to the patient.*"

— Warren Buffett

Why Mindset Matters More Than Strategy in a Bear Market

A bear market doesn't just test your **investment strategy**—it tests your **psychological strength**.

When stocks crash, real estate prices drop, and news headlines scream **"Worst Recession in Decades!"**, most investors **panic and make costly mistakes**.

The truth? **Your ability to stay calm, rational, and disciplined is what separates winners from losers.**

In this chapter, we'll cover:

✅ **How to develop an unshakable bear market mindset.**

✅ **The biggest psychological mistakes investors make in downturns.**

✅ **Mental strategies to stay focused when markets crash.**

How Fear & Greed Control Investor Behavior

📉 Fear in Bear Markets (The Emotional Sell-Off)

• As stocks and real estate drop, **investors panic-sell at the worst possible time.**

• They assume, *"It will never recover,"* and lock in permanent losses.

• Fear-driven selling is **why markets crash faster than they rise.**

📈 Greed in Bull Markets (The Buying Frenzy)

• In bull markets, investors **chase overpriced assets**, believing prices will rise forever.

• They ignore fundamentals and buy based on hype, leading to market bubbles.

📌 **Lesson:** *Fear makes investors sell at the bottom. Greed makes them buy at the top. The key to wealth is avoiding both extremes.*

The Three Biggest Mental Mistakes Investors Make in Bear Markets

1. Selling at the Bottom (Locking in Permanent Losses)

- Most investors can't handle watching their portfolio drop **30-50%**, so they **sell in panic mode**.

- But history shows **every bear market eventually recovers**—those who hold on see massive gains.

📌 **How to Overcome It:**

✅ Remind yourself that **bear markets are temporary, but losses are permanent if you sell.**

✅ Look at past market crashes—**the S&P 500 has recovered from every single one.**

2. Trying to Time the Exact Bottom

- Investors want to **buy at the perfect low**, but no one can predict it.

- Instead of buying when assets are cheap, they **wait too long and miss the recovery.**

📌 **How to Overcome It:**

✅ Use **Dollar-Cost Averaging (DCA)**—buy gradually as prices drop.

✅ Focus on **valuations, not short-term price movements.**

3. Letting News Headlines Control Their Decisions

- The media **exaggerates fear in bear markets** because panic gets more views.

- Headlines like **"This Time Is Different"** and **"The Market Will Never Recover"** are designed to scare you.

📌 How to Overcome It:

✅ Turn off financial news—**it fuels emotional decision-making.**

✅ Read history—**markets have always recovered, no matter how bad the headlines sounded.**

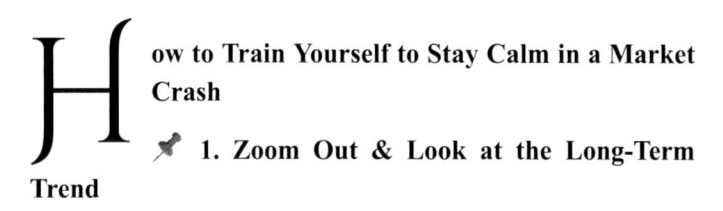

How to Train Yourself to Stay Calm in a Market Crash

📌 1. Zoom Out & Look at the Long-Term Trend

✅ The S&P 500 has had **dozens of crashes**, but the long-term trend is **UP.**

✅ If you look at a **30-year stock market chart**, bear markets are just bumps in the road.

📌 2. Focus on Buying Quality, Not Chasing Prices

✅ Instead of worrying about the **perfect entry price**, focus on **buying strong assets at a discount.**

✅ **Bear markets create millionaires**—but only for those who buy when prices are low.

📌 3. Study How the Wealthy Handle Market Crashes

✅ **Warren Buffett bought stocks aggressively in 2008** when everyone else was panicking.

✅ **Ray Dalio hedges with gold and bonds**, but still invests in equities long-term.

✅ The richest investors **use downturns to expand their wealth**, while average investors panic.

📌 **4. Have a Bear Market Plan Before It Happens**

✅ Know exactly **what you will buy and at what price** before a recession hits.

✅ Keep a list of **strong stocks, real estate deals, and assets** you want to own.

📌 **5. Stay Busy & Avoid Watching the Markets Daily**

✅ Checking your portfolio **every 5 minutes increases stress and fear.**

✅ Set a **schedule for reviewing your investments once per month.**

Why Patience Wins in Bear Markets

🚀 **The 2008 Financial Crisis Example:**

• In 2008, investors **sold stocks in fear**, believing markets would never recover.

• The S&P 500 fell **-57%**, but those who held on **saw 400%+ returns over the next decade.**

🚀 **The COVID-19 Crash Example:**

• In March 2020, the market **dropped 35% in weeks**—many panic-sold.

- By 2021, the market **hit new all-time highs**, and patient investors made huge gains.

📌 **Lesson:** *Every market crash looks like "the end of the world" at the time—but it never is. Patience and discipline always pay off.*

My Opinion

I've seen too many investors **self-destruct in bear markets**—not because they had bad investments, but because they **let emotions control their decisions.**

In my opinion, **surviving and thriving in downturns is more about mental strength than financial knowledge.** If you can:

✅ **Control your emotions.**

✅ **Stay patient when others panic.**

✅ **Focus on buying assets when they're cheap.**

Then you will **come out of every bear market wealthier than before.**

If you learn only one thing from this chapter, let it be this: **Most investors lose money in bear markets not because they pick bad assets, but because they can't handle short-term pain.** Master your mindset, and you'll master the market.

In the next chapter, we'll cover **how to position yourself for the next bull market—and turn everything you've learned into a long-term wealth-building strategy.**

📌 SECTION VI: CASE STUDIES & EXECUTION PLAN

CHAPTER 20: POSITIONING FOR THE NEXT BULL MARKET – TURNING CRISIS INTO WEALTH

"The stock market is designed to transfer money from the impatient to the patient."

— Warren Buffett

Why the Best Time to Prepare for a Bull Market Is During a Bear Market

Most investors only think about **bull markets when stocks are already rising**. By then, it's too late—the best deals are gone, and you're **chasing overpriced assets** like everyone else.

The secret to making life-changing wealth? **Position yourself while prices are still low.**

Bear markets are temporary, but **the wealth-building opportunities they create last for decades**—if you know how to prepare.

In this chapter, we'll cover:

✅ **How to recognize when a bull market is coming.**

☑ **The best investments to buy before the next uptrend.**

☑ **How to build a long-term wealth strategy to maximize gains.**

How to Recognize When a Bull Market Is Coming

Bear markets create maximum fear.

Bull markets begin when fear turns into opportunity.

Key Signs the Market Is Bottoming & a Bull Run Is Near

📌 **1. The Federal Reserve Stops Raising Interest Rates**

• When the Fed **pauses or cuts rates**, markets react positively.

• Lower rates mean **cheaper borrowing, higher stock prices, and stronger economic growth.**

📌 **2. Unemployment Peaking & Economic Data Improving**

• Recessions **increase layoffs**, but bull markets begin **as hiring starts again.**

• Watch **job reports and GDP growth**—when they improve, the worst is over.

📌 **3. Market Sentiment Turns from Fear to Neutral**

• **Fear & Greed Index** rises from **extreme fear (<20) to neutral (>50).**

- **Media stops predicting total collapse** and starts seeing opportunities.

📌 4. Big Investors Start Buying Again

- When hedge funds and institutions **move money into stocks, real estate, and crypto**, the bull market is forming.

- Insider buying increases—**CEOs and executives start buying their own stock.**

📌 5. Quality Stocks & Assets Begin Recovering First

- **Defensive stocks stop falling**, and **growth stocks start rising gradually.**

- Small-cap stocks and tech **start outperforming the market.**

📌 *Lesson: The early signs of a bull market appear when most investors are still too scared to buy. The biggest profits go to those who invest before the crowd realizes the uptrend has begun.*

The Best Investments to Buy Before the Next Bull Market

1. High-Quality Stocks at Bear Market Discounts

- The best stocks of the next bull run **are the ones that survived the bear market.**

- **Look for:**

✅ **Profitable, cash-rich companies** (avoid companies that need debt to survive).

✅ **Industries with long-term growth trends** (AI, renewable energy, tech, healthcare).

✅ **Stocks that held up well in the bear market**—they will likely **lead the next rally.**

📌 **Best Examples from Past Bull Markets:**

• 2008 Crash: **Amazon (AMZN) fell to $35, later rose to $3,500.**

• 2020 Crash: **Tesla (TSLA) dropped to $85, later surged to $1,200.**

🚫 **What to Avoid:**

❌ Speculative stocks that rely on hype (meme stocks, unprofitable companies).

❌ Companies drowning in debt that barely survived the recession.

2. Growth Stocks That Got Oversold

• Growth stocks get **crushed in bear markets** but **rise the fastest in bull markets.**

• Look for **companies with strong revenue, solid balance sheets, and future growth potential.**

📌 **Best Growth Sectors for the Next Bull Market:**

✅ **Artificial Intelligence (AI) & Cloud Computing** – Microsoft (MSFT), NVIDIA (NVDA), Snowflake (SNOW).

✅ **Renewable Energy & EVs** – Tesla (TSLA), Enphase Energy (ENPH), NextEra Energy (NEE).

☑ **Healthcare & Biotech** – Pfizer (PFE), Moderna (MRNA), CRISPR Therapeutics (CRSP).

🚫 **What to Avoid:**

✘ Unprofitable tech stocks that burned cash in the last cycle.

✘ Stocks that were **overhyped in the last bull market** but failed to grow (Peloton, Zoom, etc.).

3. Real Estate in Rebounding Markets

• **Housing prices usually bottom out before a bull market begins.**

• As the economy **recovers and rates stabilize, real estate demand surges.**

📌 **Best Real Estate Plays for a Bull Market:**

☑ **Multi-family apartments** – Demand rises as renters look for stable housing.

☑ **Commercial real estate rebound** – Warehouses, logistics centers, and retail.

☑ **Sunbelt & high-growth cities** – Florida, Texas, Arizona attract new buyers.

🚫 **What to Avoid:**

✘ High-priced real estate in slow-growth cities.

✘ Overleveraged properties that struggle with cash flow.

. . .

4. Crypto's Strongest Survivors

- In every crypto bear market, **most altcoins die, but Bitcoin & Ethereum survive.**
- Institutions accumulate BTC & ETH before the next cycle.

📌 **Best Crypto Investments for a New Bull Market:**

✅ **Bitcoin (BTC)** – Digital gold, the safest long-term bet.

✅ **Ethereum (ETH)** – Powers smart contracts, DeFi, and Web3.

✅ **Blue-chip altcoins with strong use cases** – Solana (SOL), Chainlink (LINK).

🚫 **What to Avoid:**

❌ Meme coins (Dogecoin, Shiba Inu) – Hype-driven, no real-world use.

❌ Small altcoins without real utility – 90% of these disappear in bear markets.

5. Commodities & Inflation-Proof Assets

- **Commodities surge in early bull markets** due to growing demand.
- **Gold, silver, and oil** often rise when the economy rebounds.

📌 **Best Inflation-Proof Investments:**

✅ **Gold & Silver** – Protects against currency devaluation.

✅ **Oil & Energy Stocks** – ExxonMobil (XOM), Chevron (CVX).

✅ **Agriculture & Food** – Wheat, soybeans, fertilizer stocks.

📌 **What to Avoid:**

❌ Overleveraged mining stocks with high debt.

How to Build a Long-Term Wealth Strategy for the Next Bull Market

📌 1. Have a Watchlist of Stocks & Assets You Want to Buy

✅ Identify **quality investments you want to own before the market turns.**

✅ Set price alerts **so you can buy when the time is right.**

📌 2. Start Buying Gradually as Sentiment Improves

✅ Use **Dollar-Cost Averaging (DCA)** to build positions over time.

✅ Buy **strong assets while they are cheap—before the crowd jumps in.**

📌 3. Stay Patient & Ignore Short-Term Noise

✅ Bull markets **don't happen overnight**—they build slowly over time.

✅ Avoid **chasing stocks too early**—accumulate while prices are still reasonable.

📌 4. Hold Your Winners & Ride the Uptrend

✅ Once a bull market starts, **let your best investments run.**

✅ Avoid **selling too early out of fear.**

My Opinion

I've seen too many investors **wait until the bull market is already here to start investing**—by then, the best opportunities are gone.

In my opinion, the biggest mistake people make is **not preparing while assets are still cheap.** If you wait until the media says, *"The recession is over!"*—you're already too late.

The best investors **position themselves early.** They:

✅ **Accumulate quality assets while they're undervalued.**

✅ **Stay patient when others are still afraid.**

✅ **Hold their investments as the bull market unfolds.**

If you do this, **the next bull market will be your biggest wealth-building opportunity yet.**

CHAPTER 21: THE 42 BULLETPROOF STRATEGIES CHECKLIST

" *A good plan violently executed now is better than a perfect plan next week.*"

— George S. Patton

How to Use This Checklist to Build Wealth in Any Market

Now that you've learned how to profit in bear markets, it's time to **turn knowledge into action.**

This chapter provides a **step-by-step checklist** covering **all 42 strategies from this book** so you can:

✅ **Apply them to your investment plan.**

✅ **Track your progress in real time.**

✅ **Make sure you're financially bulletproof in every market cycle.**

. . .

The 42 Bulletproof Strategies for Profiting in Bear Markets

📌 MINDSET & PREPARATION (The Foundation for Success)

1. Accept that **bear markets are inevitable** and plan accordingly.

2. Develop a **long-term investing mindset**—focus on wealth accumulation, not short-term fear.

3. Learn from history—**every bear market has led to new all-time highs.**

4. Avoid emotional decisions—**turn off financial news when panic takes over.**

5. Write down your **bear market plan in advance** so you don't react emotionally.

6. Keep **cash reserves ready** to buy assets at a discount.

7. Identify **the right moment to switch from defense to offense.**

8. Build a **watchlist of quality assets** you want to buy during downturns.

9. Set up **price alerts** to catch investment opportunities.

10. Focus on **increasing your income streams** so you have more money to invest.

. . .

DEFENSIVE STRATEGIES (Protecting Your Wealth)

11 Reduce exposure to **high-risk speculative assets** before a bear market hits.

12 Increase cash holdings **as the market starts showing weakness.**

13 Shift to **defensive stocks** like consumer staples, utilities, and healthcare.

14 Pay down **high-interest debt** to reduce financial stress.

15 Maintain a **6-12 month emergency fund** to avoid forced selling.

16 Hedge your portfolio with **gold, silver, and commodities.**

17 Increase exposure to **bonds when interest rates are peaking.**

18 Use **dividend stocks** to generate passive income during downturns.

19 Consider **REITs (Real Estate Investment Trusts)** for steady cash flow.

20 Use **options strategies like protective puts** to hedge against crashes.

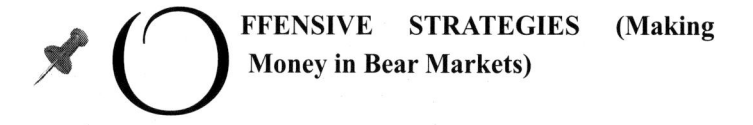

OFFENSIVE STRATEGIES (Making Money in Bear Markets)

2.1 Buy **stocks of strong, profitable companies** at bear market discounts.

2.2 Invest in **growth stocks** that are temporarily oversold.

2.3 Use **Dollar-Cost Averaging (DCA)** to buy assets gradually.

2.4 Short sell **overvalued stocks that are likely to drop further.**

2.5 Use **put options to profit from falling markets.**

2.6 Buy **defensive real estate at recession-level prices.**

2.7 Target **foreclosures and distressed properties** in housing downturns.

2.8 Consider **high-quality cryptocurrency assets** that will survive the next cycle.

2.9 Take advantage of **commercial real estate opportunities** in economic downturns.

3.0 Sell cash-secured puts on **stocks you want to own at lower prices.**

POSITIONING FOR THE NEXT BULL MARKET

3.1 Watch for signs of **market bottoming** (Fed rate cuts, improved job market, etc.).

3.2 Follow **big investors and hedge funds**—they buy before the crowd.

3.3 Rotate back into **high-growth sectors** before the next uptrend.

Bear Market Millionaire: 42 Bulletproof Strategies to Profit from …

34 Buy **real estate before interest rates start dropping again.**

35 Accumulate **crypto before the next bull cycle begins.**

36 Invest in **commodities (oil, gold, silver) as inflation stabilizes.**

37 Hold onto **high-quality assets for the long run**—don't sell too early.

38 Rebalance your portfolio **as the economy shifts back into growth mode.**

39 Increase stock exposure when **market sentiment shifts from fear to optimism.**

40 Focus on **compound growth—reinvest dividends and let assets appreciate.**

41 Use leverage **wisely and strategically** when markets are recovering.

42 Stay patient—**bull markets take time to build, but the rewards are huge.**

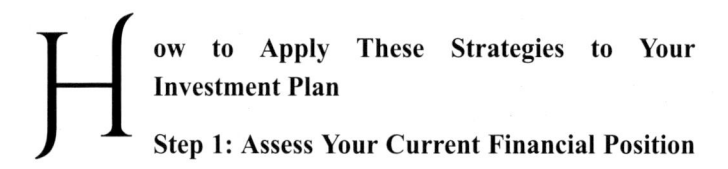

How to Apply These Strategies to Your Investment Plan

Step 1: Assess Your Current Financial Position

◆ How much **cash** do you have available to invest?

◆ Are you **holding too much risk** in speculative assets?

◆ Do you have an **emergency fund to avoid forced selling?**

Step 2: Identify Where You Are in the Market Cycle

◆ Is the **economy still declining** (stay defensive), or are we **near a bottom** (start buying)?

◆ Are interest rates **rising or stabilizing**?

◆ Are big investors **buying or selling**?

Step 3: Build Your Defensive Position

◆ Shift part of your portfolio into **cash, bonds, dividend stocks, and commodities.**

◆ Hedge with **put options, gold, and inflation-resistant assets.**

◆ Pay down **high-interest debt and strengthen your cash flow.**

Step 4: Plan Your Offensive Strategy

◆ Make a **list of stocks, real estate, and cryptos** you want to buy.

◆ Set **buy targets based on valuations, not emotions.**

◆ Start buying gradually—**don't try to time the exact bottom.**

Step 5: Stay Disciplined & Track Your Progress

◆ Stick to your **plan regardless of market noise.**

◆ Track your investments **monthly to see if adjustments are needed.**

◆ Keep a **long-term perspective**—bear markets don't last forever.

. . .

Tracking Your Progress in Real Time

📌 How to Know If You're on Track:

✅ You **are not panic-selling**—you are **buying or holding quality assets.**

✅ You have **enough cash to invest when opportunities arise.**

✅ You are **earning passive income** from dividends, real estate, or other sources.

✅ You are **not relying on news headlines** to make investment decisions.

✅ You are positioned for **long-term wealth creation, not short-term emotions.**

My Opinion

I've seen **too many investors lose wealth in bear markets** simply because they didn't have a plan. They sold at the worst times, bought at the wrong moments, and **let emotions dictate their financial future.**

In my opinion, **the strategies in this book give you an unfair advantage.** While most people panic, you'll know exactly what to do. While others **wait for the economy to "feel good" again,** you'll already be positioned for the next bull run.

This checklist is **your personal bear market playbook**—use it wisely, and you won't just survive downturns. You'll emerge from them **wealthier than ever before.**

CHAPTER 22: CREATING YOUR BEAR MARKET ACTION PLAN – STEP-BY-STEP GUIDE TO PROFITING IN DOWNTURNS

"*By failing to prepare, you are preparing to fail.*"
— Benjamin Franklin

Why You Need a Bear Market Action Plan

Most investors **react emotionally** when the market crashes. They panic-sell, hesitate to buy, or freeze in fear—only to regret their decisions when the bull market returns.

The **wealthiest investors do the opposite**. They don't react —they **execute a pre-planned strategy** with confidence.

This chapter provides a **step-by-step guide to preparing for bear markets** so you always know:

✅ **When to buy, when to hold, and when to exit.**

✅ **How to position your portfolio for long-term success.**

✅ **How to stay calm, take action, and come out wealthier than before.**

. . .

Step 1: Assess Your Current Financial Position

Before making investment moves, **take stock of where you stand.**

📌 **Key Questions to Ask Yourself:**

◆ **How much cash do I have available to invest?**

◆ **Do I have high-interest debt that should be paid down first?**

◆ **How much risk am I currently exposed to in my portfolio?**

◆ **Do I have an emergency fund to cover 6-12 months of expenses?**

◆ **Am I mentally prepared to hold through market volatility?**

🚨 **Warning:** If you have **no emergency fund and high-interest debt**, focus on fixing those first before investing aggressively in a downturn.

Step 2: Define Your Investment Goals

📌 **Ask Yourself:**

✅ **What's my primary goal?** (Long-term wealth, passive income, growth, etc.)

✅ **How much risk can I handle?** (Aggressive, moderate, or conservative?)

✅ **Do I want active or passive investments?** (Hands-on trading vs. buy-and-hold.)

Your **answers will shape your investment strategy.**

🚀 **Example:**

• **If you want passive income**, focus on **dividend stocks, REITs, and bonds.**

• **If you want growth**, buy **tech stocks, crypto, and undervalued assets.**

• **If you want security**, hold **gold, cash, and defensive stocks.**

📌 **Lesson:** *Your strategy must align with your financial goals.*

Step 3: Set Your Bear Market Buying Strategy

When assets drop in price, **you need a plan for buying opportunities.**

💰 **How to Decide What to Buy**

✅ **Stocks:** Focus on **blue-chip companies, dividend stocks, and tech leaders.**

✅ **Real Estate:** Look for **foreclosures, motivated sellers, and rental properties.**

✅ **Crypto:** Accumulate **Bitcoin (BTC) & Ethereum (ETH) while prices are low.**

✅ **Gold & Commodities:** Hedge against inflation and uncertainty.

📈 **When to Buy (Bear Market Indicators)**

Bear Market Millionaire: 42 Bulletproof Strategies to Profit from ...

📌 **1. Stock Market Down 20%+ from Highs** → Start accumulating.

📌 **2. Fear & Greed Index Below 20** → Sentiment is at extreme fear.

📌 **3. Federal Reserve Signals Rate Cuts** → Markets anticipate recovery.

📌 **4. Unemployment Peaking** → The worst of the recession is likely over.

🛒 **How to Buy (Execution Strategy)**

📌 **Dollar-Cost Averaging (DCA)** – Buy in small amounts **over time** to avoid mistiming the bottom.

📌 **Lump Sum Buying** – If the market **crashes 40-50%**, consider buying aggressively.

📌 **Buy the Strongest Assets First** – Focus on **financially healthy companies** that will lead the recovery.

📌 **Lesson:** *Have a **clear, disciplined strategy** for buying in a bear market—don't leave it to emotions.*

Step 4: Decide When to Hold and When to Exit

📌 **Holding Strategy (Long-Term Investing)**

✅ Hold **quality assets for the long haul**—don't sell out of fear.

✅ **Ignore short-term noise**—bear markets are temporary.

✅ **Reinvest dividends** to compound wealth over time.

📌 **When to Sell (Exiting at the Right Time)**

✖ **Sell overvalued assets when they reach excessive greed levels.**

✖ **Sell if a company's fundamentals deteriorate (rising debt, falling revenue).**

✖ **Sell if you reach your profit target and want to rebalance your portfolio.**

📌 **Lesson:** *Buy with a plan, hold with patience, and sell when the time is right—not out of panic.*

Step 5: Build a Diversified Portfolio for Long-Term Success

The best bear market strategy balances **offense (growth) and defense (protection).**

📌 **Example of a Balanced Bear Market Portfolio:**

☑ **30% Defensive Stocks** – Healthcare, consumer staples, utilities.

☑ **20% Growth Stocks** – Tech, AI, emerging industries.

☑ **15% Dividend Stocks** – Cash flow generators.

☑ **10% Bonds** – Stability and income.

☑ **10% Commodities (Gold, Silver, Oil)** – Inflation hedge.

☑ **10% Cash Reserves** – Ready to deploy on great deals.

☑ **5% Crypto (BTC, ETH)** – Long-term hedge.

📌 **Lesson:** *A well-balanced portfolio allows you to* **survive downturns** *and* **thrive in the recovery.** *Don't put all your money into one asset class.*

Step 6: Track Your Progress & Adjust as Needed

How to Monitor Your Plan:

☑ **Review your portfolio monthly**—avoid checking it daily to reduce stress.

☑ **Rebalance if necessary**—if an asset class becomes overexposed, adjust.

☑ **Stay patient**—bear markets take time to play out.

Signs You're on Track:

☑ You are **buying assets gradually as prices drop.**

☑ You are **not panic-selling.**

☑ You are **generating cash flow from dividends, bonds, or real estate.**

☑ You have **cash available for opportunities.**

📌 *Lesson: Stick to your plan, track your investments, and stay patient—wealth builds over time.*

My Opinion

I've seen too many investors **panic in bear markets** because they didn't have a plan. They sold too early, missed buying opportunities, or got wiped out due to poor risk management.

In my opinion, **the best way to win in bear markets is to prepare before they happen.** Having a written plan eliminates emotional decision-making** and allows you to act with confidence when others are scared.

✅ **Defend when the market is weak, attack when it's strong.**

✅ **Buy undervalued assets while others panic.**

✅ **Hold long-term and let time work in your favor.**

If you follow this **Bear Market Action Plan**, you won't just survive downturns—you'll thrive and come out wealthier than before.

CHAPTER 23: AVOIDING COMMON MISTAKES & PSYCHOLOGICAL PITFALLS

"*Successful investing is not about avoiding risk—it's about managing it.*"

— Howard Marks

Why Most Investors Fail in Bear Markets

Investing in bear markets isn't just about **knowing what to do**—it's about **avoiding what not to do.**

Most investors **lose money not because they pick bad assets, but because they let emotions control their decisions.** They panic-sell, hesitate to buy, and let fear override logic.

This chapter will help you:

✅ Avoid the biggest bear market investing mistakes.

✅ Stay emotionally disciplined when markets are crashing.

✅ Overcome analysis paralysis and take action.

. . .

The Most Costly Mistakes Bear Market Investors Make

🪨 Mistake #1: Selling in Panic Instead of Holding Strong Assets

- When the market crashes, **fear takes over, and investors sell at the bottom.**

- They think they're "cutting losses" when in reality, **they're locking in permanent losses.**

📌 Example:

- In 2008, investors panic-sold **Apple (AAPL) at $12 per share**—years later, it hit **$400+ per share.**

- In 2020, many sold **Tesla (TSLA) at $85**, missing its **1,000%+ rise.**

✅ How to Avoid It:

- Understand that **bear markets are temporary, but selling creates permanent losses.**

- Ask yourself: *"If I sell now, will I regret it when the market recovers?"*

✴️ Mistake #2: Waiting for the "Perfect" Bottom Instead of Buying Gradually

- Some investors **refuse to buy until they can time the absolute bottom.**

- They watch markets recover, hesitate too long, and miss the best deals.

📌 Example:

• In 2020, many investors **waited for Bitcoin to drop below $3,000**—it never did.

• In 2009, investors **waited for stocks to go even lower**—the market recovered instead.

✅ How to Avoid It:

• Use **Dollar-Cost Averaging (DCA)**—buy in small amounts over time instead of trying to time the bottom.

• Focus on **valuations, not price predictions.**

Mistake #3: Letting Fearful News Headlines Control Your Decisions

• The media **profits from fear**—headlines exaggerate market crashes.

• Investors who rely on news **make emotional, reactionary decisions.**

📌 Example:

• In 2008, headlines screamed **"This is the next Great Depression!"**—yet the market fully recovered.

• In 2020, media said **"The economy may never recover!"**—yet stocks hit all-time highs in 2021.

✅ How to Avoid It:

• Turn off financial news **when markets crash**—focus on long-term trends.

- Study past bear markets **to see how recoveries always happen.**

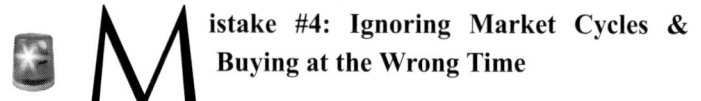

Mistake #4: Ignoring Market Cycles & Buying at the Wrong Time

- Some investors **buy too aggressively in bull markets** and **ignore bargains in bear markets.**

- They chase hype when stocks are expensive, but freeze when they're cheap.

📌 Example:

- People **bought Bitcoin at $69,000 in 2021** (FOMO) but ignored it at **$16,000 in 2022.**

- Many **bought tech stocks at record highs in 2021**, but feared buying them after they dropped 50% in 2022.

✅ How to Avoid It:

- Follow **Warren Buffett's rule: "Be fearful when others are greedy, and greedy when others are fearful."**

- **Invest when valuations are low, not when hype is high.**

Mistake #5: Overleveraging & Using Too Much Debt

- Some investors **use margin (borrowed money) to buy stocks**, only to get wiped out in crashes.

- Others **take on risky real estate debt, assuming markets will always rise.**

📌 **Example:**

• In 2008, **millions of homeowners lost properties** because they overleveraged.

• In 2022, **overleveraged crypto investors got wiped out** as Bitcoin crashed 75%.

✅ **How to Avoid It:**

• Use **little or no leverage**—especially in bear markets.

• Avoid **taking on debt unless you have strong cash flow to cover it.**

How to Stay Emotionally Disciplined in a Bear Market

1. Reframe Bear Markets as Buying Opportunities

• Instead of **fearing downturns, view them as the best time to invest.**

• Remind yourself: **Bear markets create millionaires—if you stay calm and buy wisely.**

📌 **Mindset Shift:**

❌ **Old Thinking:** *"I'm afraid the market will drop more."*

✅ **New Thinking:** *"Prices are lower than they were last year—I'm getting a discount."*

. . .

2. Have a Written Investment Plan to Follow

- Making decisions **in the moment leads to emotional mistakes.**
- A written plan **keeps you disciplined.**

📌 **Write Down:**

- ✅ Your **buying strategy** (what assets you'll buy & when).
- ✅ Your **holding strategy** (how long you'll stay invested).
- ✅ Your **selling strategy** (when to take profits or rebalance).

3. Avoid Checking Your Portfolio Too Often

- **Watching every price move increases stress and leads to bad decisions.**
- If you're a long-term investor, **checking once a month is enough.**

📌 **Rule of Thumb:**

- ◆ **Day traders check markets daily.**
- ◆ **Long-term investors check monthly or quarterly.**

4. Surround Yourself with Rational Investors

- If your **friends, social media, or news sources** constantly spread fear, **you'll absorb their** emotions.

- Instead, **learn from successful long-term investors** (Buffett, Dalio, Marks).

📌 **Tip:** Follow investors who **stay calm, buy in downturns, and focus on fundamentals.**

Overcoming Analysis Paralysis & Taking Action

🖼️ Many investors get stuck overthinking and never take action.

Why Analysis Paralysis Happens:

❌ They want the **perfect investment strategy** (which doesn't exist).

❌ They overanalyze data **instead of making small moves.**

❌ They fear making a mistake **so they do nothing.**

✅ **How to Overcome It:**

📌 **1. Set a deadline for making decisions.** (Example: "I will buy my first stock this month.")

📌 **2. Start small—invest in just one quality asset to build confidence.**

📌 **3. Remember, NOT investing is also a risk—you miss out on compounding growth.**

. . .

My Opinion

I've seen investors **lose more money from emotional mistakes than from bad investments.** They sell too soon, wait too long, or get stuck in analysis paralysis.

In my opinion, the best investors:

☑ **Understand that market crashes are normal and temporary.**

☑ **Buy assets when they're cheap—even when it feels uncomfortable.**

☑ **Stick to a plan and avoid making decisions based on emotions.**

If you can **control your emotions, avoid common mistakes, and take action when others hesitate,** you'll build wealth in every market cycle.

CHAPTER 24: PREPARING FOR THE NEXT RECESSION—TODAY

"*History doesn't repeat itself, but it often rhymes.*"
— Mark Twain

Why Recessions & Bear Markets Will Always Come Back

Recessions are not a matter of *if*—they are a matter of *when*.

Most people believe **financial crises are rare**, but history tells a different story. On average, the U.S. experiences a **recession every 6-10 years.**

📉 **Major Recessions & Bear Markets in the Last Century:**

• **1929-1932 (Great Depression):** Stock market dropped **-89%.**

• **1973-1974 (Oil Crisis):** Inflation soared, stocks fell **-48%.**

• **2000-2002 (Dot-Com Crash):** Overhyped tech stocks collapsed **-50-80%.**

- **2008-2009 (Global Financial Crisis):** Housing bubble burst, S&P 500 fell **-57%**.

- **2020 (COVID-19 Crash):** Fastest crash in history (-35% in one month), followed by rapid recovery.

📌 **Lesson:** *Economic crashes are part of the cycle. If you're not prepared, you'll suffer. If you are, you'll thrive.*

How to Build Long-Term Wealth Using Bear Market Cycles

Bear markets **destroy wealth for the unprepared**—but create *massive opportunities* for those who are ready.

The wealthiest investors use **market cycles to their advantage** by following these key principles:

1. Accept That Bear Markets Are Normal

- Most people **fear market crashes** because they don't understand them.

- The reality? **Markets always recover and reach new highs.**

📌 **Example:**

- The S&P 500 has had **dozens of crashes**, but it has **always rebounded to all-time highs.**

📌 **How to Apply It:**

☑ **Stay invested**—don't sell out of fear.

☑ **Use bear markets as buying opportunities.**

2. Keep Cash Ready to Buy at Rock-Bottom Prices

• The biggest mistake investors make? **Having no cash when prices are cheap.**

• The best deals happen **when everyone else is panicking.**

📌 Example:

• Warren Buffett **always keeps cash reserves** so he can buy great stocks at discounts.

📌 How to Apply It:

☑ Keep **10-30% of your portfolio in cash** to deploy in bear markets.

☑ Use **high-yield savings accounts or short-term bonds** for cash reserves.

3. Focus on Owning High-Quality Assets

• Not all stocks, real estate, or crypto will survive downturns.

• Buy **strong, cash-flowing assets** that will **outlast the recession.**

📌 Example:

• In 2008, **companies with high debt failed**—but cash-rich businesses like Apple (AAPL) thrived.

📌 How to Apply It:

☑ Own **blue-chip stocks, real estate, and dividend investments.**

☑ Avoid **companies that rely on hype, debt, or speculation.**

4. Buy in Bear Markets, Sell in Bull Markets

• Most investors do the opposite—they buy in euphoria and sell in fear.

• The best strategy? **Buy when prices are low, sell when greed returns.**

📌 **Example:**

• In 2020, Amazon (AMZN) dropped to **$1,600 per share**—it later surged above **$3,500.**

📌 **How to Apply It:**

☑ **Buy assets gradually as they drop** (Dollar-Cost Averaging).

☑ **Take profits when markets become irrationally overvalued.**

5. Build Passive Income Streams to Survive Recessions

• If a recession hits, **having multiple income sources protects you.**

• Passive income from **dividends, rental properties, or side businesses** keeps cash flowing.

📌 Example:

- During the 2008 crash, **landlords with rental income survived better than those relying only on a job.**

📌 How to Apply It:

☑ Own **dividend stocks that pay income even in bear markets.**

☑ Build **real estate cash flow or online businesses for** additional revenue.

6. Stay Away from High Debt & Overleveraging

- In recessions, **debt becomes a wealth killer.**
- Many people lost their homes in 2008 **because they were overleveraged.**

📌 Example:

- Homeowners with **adjustable-rate mortgages (ARMs) in 2008** saw payments skyrocket when the crisis hit.

📌 How to Apply It:

☑ Keep **debt-to-income ratios low**—avoid excessive borrowing.

☑ Use **fixed-rate mortgages** instead of risky adjustable loans.

. . .

7. Develop a Permanent Recession-Resilient Mindset

• The economy **will always have crashes and recoveries.**

• If you **mentally prepare now**, you won't panic when the next one happens.

📌 **Mindset Shift:**

❌ **Old Thinking:** "This recession is different—it's the worst ever."

☑ **New Thinking:** "Every recession in history has ended with new market highs."

📌 **How to Apply It:**

☑ Train yourself to **see recessions as wealth-building moments.**

☑ Stop reacting emotionally—**execute your pre-planned strategy.**

How to Prepare for the Next Recession—Starting Today

📌 **1. Set Up Your Financial Safety Net**

☑ **Build a 6-12 month emergency fund** (cash reserves).

☑ **Pay down high-interest debt** before the economy weakens.

✅ **Ensure multiple income streams** so you're not reliant on one job.

📌 2. Position Your Portfolio for Bear Markets

✅ Allocate **10-30% cash** to buy assets when prices drop.

✅ Invest in **defensive assets** (dividends, real estate, gold, bonds).

✅ Identify **stocks, real estate, and crypto you want to buy in downturns.**

📌 3. Train Your Mindset for Market Crashes

✅ Study **past recessions** to understand they are temporary.

✅ Follow **long-term investors, not panic-driven news headlines.**

✅ Stay patient—**bear markets last months or years, but recoveries bring massive wealth.**

📌 4. Have a Written Investment Plan

✅ Define your **buying strategy** (when & what to buy).

✅ Have **rules for selling & rebalancing** when markets recover.

✅ Review and adjust **quarterly, not daily.**

My Opinion

I've seen investors **lose fortunes because they weren't prepared for recessions.** But I've also seen **ordinary people become wealthy** by using bear markets to their advantage.

In my opinion, the biggest mistake investors make is **acting like recessions won't happen.**

The reality?

☑ **Crashes are normal.**

☑ **Markets always recover.**

☑ **The best time to prepare is BEFORE the downturn happens.**

If you **apply what you've learned in this book**, you won't just survive the next recession—you'll thrive and come out richer than before.

CHAPTER 25: FINAL WORDS – TURNING CHAOS INTO WEALTH

"The stock market is filled with individuals who know the price of everything, but the value of nothing."

— Philip Fisher

The Ultimate Lesson: Chaos Creates Opportunity

Every bear market feels like **the end of the world** at the time. People panic, the media spreads fear, and investors rush to sell their assets. But here's what separates the wealthy from the average investor:

✅ **They see financial chaos as a wealth-building opportunity.**

✅ **They don't react emotionally—they execute a well-planned strategy.**

✅ **They prepare before downturns happen, not when it's too late.**

This book wasn't just about **surviving bear markets**—it was about **thriving in them.**

If you apply what you've learned, you'll never fear another recession again. Instead, you'll **welcome downturns as chances to grow your wealth while others panic.**

The Key Lessons from This Book

📌 1. Bear Markets & Recessions Are Inevitable—Prepare Now

- Every 6-10 years, a new crisis will come. Don't be surprised—be ready.

- Market cycles are normal. **History shows that crashes always recover.**

📌 2. The Best Time to Invest Is When Everyone Else Is Afraid

- Fear creates **once-in-a-lifetime buying opportunities** for those who are prepared.

- **Wealth is transferred from emotional investors to rational investors.**

📌 3. Have a Bear Market Playbook Ready Before the Crash

- Never **wait for the crisis to hit** before deciding what to do.

- Keep **cash reserves**, identify **buying opportunities**, and execute **without emotion.**

📌 4. Build Passive Income Streams to Stay Resilient

- Recessions hit people hardest when they **only rely on one income source.**
- **Dividend stocks, real estate, and online businesses create financial security.**

📌 5. Own Assets That Survive & Thrive in Downturns

- **Buy stocks of profitable companies, defensive sectors, and commodities.**
- **Invest in real estate that generates positive cash flow.**
- **Avoid debt-heavy, speculative assets that collapse in recessions.**

📌 6. The Biggest Mistakes Are Emotional, Not Financial

- Most investors **sell at the bottom and buy at the top** due to fear and greed.
- Avoid **checking your portfolio daily**—market noise leads to panic decisions.

📌 7. The Next Bull Market Will Be Born in the Next Bear Market

- The smartest investors **start accumulating assets before recoveries begin.**
- Markets always **go higher in the long run—buy when prices are cheap.**

. . .

How to Think Like a Bear Market Millionaire—Forever

The wealthiest investors don't have secret formulas. They simply think differently.

Here's how to adopt the **Bear Market Millionaire mindset** for the rest of your life:

◆ 1. Become a Long-Term Thinker

- Ignore **short-term noise**—bear markets are temporary, but wealth lasts forever.

- Make decisions **based on data and strategy, not emotion.**

◆ 2. Focus on Value, Not Price

- A stock dropping **doesn't mean it's a bad investment.**

- A real estate deal **isn't a bargain if it won't generate cash flow.**

◆ 3. Always Keep Cash Ready for Market Crashes

- **Don't go all-in during bull markets**—save cash for downturns.

- **Cash is not just an asset—it's an opportunity weapon.**

◆ 4. Have the Courage to Buy When Others Are Afraid

- If you feel scared to invest, **that's usually the best time to buy.**

- Every market crash **has made millionaires out of those who stayed calm.**

Bear Market Millionaire: 42 Bulletproof Strategies to Profit from ...

🔸 5. Avoid the Herd—Think Independently

• **If everyone is euphoric, be cautious.**

• **If everyone is panicking, start buying.**

🚀 **Lesson:** *The world rewards those who prepare. If you make these principles part of your financial strategy, every crisis will be an opportunity—not a threat.*

Your Next Steps to Recession-Proof Your Wealth

🚀 Step 1: Review Your Bear Market Playbook

🔸 Do you have **an emergency fund?**

🔸 Do you have **cash reserves ready to invest?**

🔸 Do you know **which assets you want to buy when markets drop?**

🚀 Step 2: Start Building Your Portfolio—Today

🔸 Begin **buying quality investments, even if the market is uncertain.**

🔸 Allocate your portfolio **based on your risk tolerance and long-term goals.**

🚀 Step 3: Strengthen Your Financial Resilience

🔸 Pay down high-interest debt—**recessions punish the overleveraged.**

🔸 Build multiple streams of income—**dividends, rental income, or side businesses.**

🚀 Step 4: Train Your Mindset for Future Market Cycles

◆ Learn from history—**study past bear markets to see the patterns.**

◆ Follow **long-term investors, not short-term traders.**

◆ Practice **controlling your emotions—your wealth depends on it.**

🚀 Step 5: Execute With Confidence & Stay the Course

◆ Bear markets **are the foundation of future bull markets.**

◆ If you stay focused and **execute what you've learned, your wealth will grow exponentially over time.**

Final Thoughts – My Opinion

I've seen investors **rise and fall in every market cycle**—and the difference between success and failure always comes down to **preparation, patience, and discipline.**

☑ The unprepared **panic and lose money.**

☑ The smart investors **execute their plan and build generational wealth.**

In my opinion, **this book gave you every tool you need to dominate bear markets.** Now, it's up to you to take action.

📌 **My final advice:** *Start today.*

☑ You don't need to be perfect—**you just need to be prepared.**

☑ You don't need to time the exact bottom—you just need to buy undervalued assets.

Bear Market Millionaire: 42 Bulletproof Strategies to Profit from ...

✅ You don't need to fear recessions—you just need to think like a Bear Market Millionaire.

The next financial crisis **isn't a disaster—it's your greatest opportunity.**

Be ready. Stay patient. And take action.

🚀 **Your journey to bear market mastery starts now.**

What's Next? Download Your Bear Market Action Plan

◆ If you want to **implement everything you've learned**, create a **customized bear market strategy** based on your portfolio and goals.

📌 **Download the Bear Market Action Plan Template & Investment Checklist** (if applicable).

◆ Print it.

◆ Review it regularly.

◆ Execute with confidence.

The future belongs to those who prepare.

Congratulations! You've completed *Bear Market Millionaire: 42 Bulletproof Strategies to Profit from Crashes, Recessions, and Economic Chaos.*

This book wasn't just about surviving downturns—it was

about **turning every financial crisis into a wealth-building opportunity.**

🚀 **Now it's time to apply what you've learned.**

See you at the top.

Manufactured by Amazon.ca
Acheson, AB